# REVELATION

*The Christian's Ultimate Victory*

JOHN MACARTHUR

THOMAS NELSON
*Since 1798*

MacArthur Bible Studies
Revelation
© 2007, John MacArthur

Requests for information should be addressed to:
HarperChristian Resources, 3900 Sparks Dr. SE, Grand Rapids, Michigan 49546

ISBN 978-0-7180-3519-8 (softcover)
ISBN 978-0-7180-3538-9 (ebook)

First Printing April 2016 / Printed in the United States of America

# CONTENTS

# INTRODUCTION TO REVELATION

Unlike most books of the Bible, this one contains its own title: "The Revelation of Jesus Christ" (1:1). This revelation was given to Him by God the Father, and it was communicated to the apostle John by an angel (1:1).

## AUTHOR AND DATE

Four times the author identifies himself as John (1:1, 4, 9; 22:8). Early tradition unanimously identified him as John the apostle, author of the fourth Gospel and three Epistles. For example, important second-century witnesses to the apostle John's authorship include Justin Martyr, Irenaeus, Clement of Alexandria, and Tertullian. Many of the book's original readers were still alive during the lifetimes of Justin Martyr and Irenaeus—both of whom held to apostolic authorship.

There are differences in style between Revelation and John's other writings, but they are insignificant and do not preclude one man from writing both. In fact, there are some striking parallels between Revelation and John's other works. Only John's Gospel and Revelation refer to Jesus Christ as the Word (19:13; John 1:2). Revelation (1:7) and John's Gospel (19:37) translate Zechariah 12:10 differently from the Septuagint, but in agreement with each other. Only Revelation and the Gospel of John describe Jesus as the Lamb (5:6, 8; John 1:29); both describe Jesus as a witness (see 1:5; John 5:31–32).

Revelation was written in the last decade of the first century (about AD 94–96), near the end of Emperor Domitian's reign (AD 81–96). Although some date it during Nero's reign (AD 54–68), their arguments are unconvincing and conflict with the view of the early church. Writing in the second century, Irenaeus declared that Revelation had been written toward the end of Domitian's reign. Later writers, such as Clement of Alexandria, Origen, Victorinus (who wrote one of the earliest commentaries on Revelation), Eusebius, and Jerome affirm the Domitian date.

The spiritual decline of the seven churches (chs. 2 and 3) also argues for the later date. Those churches were strong and spiritually healthy in the mid-60s, when Paul last ministered in Asia Minor. The brief time between Paul's ministry there and the end of Nero's reign was too short for such a decline to have occurred. The longer time gap also explains the rise of the heretical sect known as the Nicolaitans (2:6, 15), who are not mentioned in Paul's letters, not even to one or more of these same churches (Ephesians). Finally, dating Revelation during

Nero's reign does not allow time for John's ministry in Asia Minor to reach the point at which the authorities would have felt the need to exile him.

## BACKGROUND AND SETTING

Revelation begins with John, the last surviving apostle and an old man, in exile on the small, barren island of Patmos, located in the Aegean Sea southwest of Ephesus. The Roman authorities had banished him there because of his faithful preaching of the gospel (1:9). While on Patmos, John received a series of visions that laid out the future history of the world.

When he was arrested, John was in Ephesus, ministering to the church there and in the surrounding cities. Seeking to strengthen those congregations that he could no longer minister to in person, and following the divine command (1:11), John addressed Revelation to them (1:4). The churches had begun to feel the effects of persecution; at least one man—probably a pastor—had already been martyred (2:13), and John himself had been exiled. But the storm of persecution was about to break in full fury upon the seven churches so dear to the apostle's heart (2:10). To those churches, Revelation provided a message of hope: God is in sovereign control of all the events of human history, and though evil often seems pervasive and wicked men all-powerful, their ultimate doom is certain. Christ will come in glory to judge and rule.

## HISTORICAL AND THEOLOGICAL THEMES

Since it is primarily prophetic, Revelation contains little historical material, other than that in chapters 1–3. The seven churches to whom the letter was addressed were existing churches in Asia Minor (modern Turkey). Apparently, they were singled out because John had ministered in them.

Revelation is first and foremost a revelation about Jesus Christ (1:1). The book depicts Him as the risen, glorified Son of God ministering among the churches (1:10–20), as "the faithful witness, the firstborn from the dead, and the ruler over the kings of the earth" (1:5), as "the Alpha and the Omega, the Beginning and the End" (1:8), as the One "who is and who was and who is to come, the Almighty" (1:8), as the First and the Last (1:11), as the Son of Man (1:13), as the One who was dead, but now is alive forevermore (1:18), as the Son of God (2:18), as the One who is holy and true (3:7), as "the Amen, the Faithful and True Witness, the Beginning of the creation of God" (3:14), as the Lion of the tribe of Judah (5:5), as the Lamb in heaven, with authority to open the title deed to the earth (6:1–8:1), as the Lamb on the throne (7:17), as the Messiah who will reign forever (11:15), as the Word of God (19:13), as the majestic King of kings and Lord of lords, returning in glorious splendor to conquer His foes (19:11–21), and as "the Root and the Offspring of David, the Bright and Morning Star" (22:16).

Many other rich theological themes find expression in Revelation. The church is warned about sin and exhorted to holiness. John's vivid pictures of worship in heaven both exhort and instruct believers. In few other books of the Bible is the ministry of angels so prominent. Revelation's primary theological contribution is to *eschatology*, that is, the doctrine of last things. In it we learn about the final political setup of the world; the last battle of human history; the career and ultimate defeat of Antichrist; Christ's thousand-year earthly kingdom; the glories of heaven and the eternal state; and the final state of the wicked and the righteous. Finally, only Daniel rivals this book in declaring that God providentially rules over the kingdoms of men and will accomplish His sovereign purposes regardless of human or demonic opposition.

## INTERPRETIVE CHALLENGES

No other New Testament book poses more serious and difficult interpretive challenges than Revelation. The book's vivid imagery and striking symbolism have produced four main interpretive approaches:

The *preterist* approach interprets Revelation as a description of first-century events in the Roman Empire (see Author and Date). This view conflicts with the book's own often-repeated claim to be prophecy (1:3; 22:7, 10, 18, 19). It is impossible to see all the events in Revelation as already fulfilled. The second coming of Christ, for example, obviously did not take place in the first century.

The *historicist* approach views Revelation as a panoramic view of church history from apostolic times to the present—seeing in the symbolism such events as the barbarian invasions of Rome, the rise of the Roman Catholic church (as well as various individual popes), the emergence of Islam, and the French Revolution. This interpretive method robs Revelation of any meaning for those to whom it was written. It also ignores the time limitations the book itself places on the unfolding events (see 11:2; 12:6, 14; 13:5). Historicism has produced many different—and often conflicting—interpretations of the actual historical events contained in Revelation.

The *idealist* approach interprets Revelation as a timeless depiction of the cosmic struggle between the forces of good and evil. In this view, the book contains neither historical allusions nor predictive prophecy. This view also ignores Revelation's prophetic character and, if carried to its logical conclusion, severs the book from any connection with actual historical events. Revelation then becomes merely a collection of stories designed to teach spiritual truth.

The *futurist* approach insists that the events of chapters 6–22 are yet future and that those chapters literally and symbolically depict actual people and events yet to appear on the world scene. It describes the events surrounding the second coming of Jesus Christ (chs. 6–19), the Millennium and final judgment (ch. 20), and the eternal state (chs. 21 and 22). Only this view does justice to Revelation's claim to be prophecy and interprets the book by the same grammatical-historical method as chapters 1–3 and the rest of Scripture.

# 1

# BACK TO THE FUTURE
*Revelation 1:1–20*

## DRAWING NEAR

On a scale of 1–10 (1 = representing "very little understanding" and 10 = "complete and full understanding"), how would you rate your current understanding of the book of Revelation and what it teaches about end-times events?

_____

_____

_____

_____

What do you hope to learn from this study?

_____

_____

_____

_____

When you think about the future of the world, are you optimistic or pessimistic? Why?

_____

_____

_____

_____

## THE CONTEXT

Many people are fascinated, even obsessed, with the future. They faithfully read their horoscopes, seek out Tarot card readers, have their palms read, feed on futuristic scientific material, or call one of the many "psychic hot lines." All such attempts to discern the future, however, are in vain. There is only One who knows and declares the future: God (Isa. 44:7; 45:21; 46:9–10). Only in Scripture can truth about the future be found.

The Old Testament prophets, particularly Isaiah, Ezekiel, Daniel, and Zechariah, provided glimpses of the future. Jesus spoke about it, as did Peter and Paul in their inspired writings. But the book of Revelation provides the most detailed look into the future in all of Scripture. The fitting capstone of God's revelation to man in the Bible, the book of Revelation unveils the future history of the world, all the way to history's climax in the return of Christ and the setting up of His glorious earthly and eternal kingdom.

The breathtaking vision of Jesus Christ that begins John's book shows Him to be the glorified Lord of the church. For persecuted believers at the end of the first century, this reminder of Christ's present ministry to them surely provided great hope and comfort. Revelation 1:19 provides a simple outline for the entire book: "the things which you have seen," refers to the vision John has just seen (ch. 1); "the things which are" denotes the letters to the churches (chs. 2–3); and "the things which will take place after this" refers to the revelation of future history (chs. 4–22). The first chapter of Revelation makes abundantly clear that Jesus Christ is the central theme of the book. It specifies that the events described lie in the future. More importantly, from a reader's perspective, it promises blessings to those who study and obey the contents of John's prophecy.

*Note:* This study of Revelation moves quickly through large passages and will only allow us to look at major themes and events. As we encounter more of the apocalyptic and cryptic language of the book of Revelation, it will not be possible to study all the symbols and meanings in depth. Be sure to use the study notes that are provided next to the passages for further interpretation of these things, or refer to my *New Testament Commentary on Revelation* (Moody Press).

## KEYS TO THE TEXT

*Revelation:* This word comes from the Greek word *apokalypsis* and means "an uncovering," "an unveiling," or "a disclosure." In the New Testament, this word describes the unveiling of spiritual truth (Rom. 16:25; Gal. 1:12; Eph. 1:17; 3:3), the revealing of the sons of God (Rom. 8:19), Christ's incarnation (Luke 2:32), and His glorious appearing at His second coming (2 Thess. 1:7; 1 Pet. 1:7). In all its uses, "revelation" refers to something or someone once hidden, becoming visible. What this book reveals or unveils is Jesus Christ in glory. Truths about Jesus and His final victory become clearly visible through this revelation.

*Apostle John:* John was an apostle and one of the three most intimate associates of Jesus (see Matt. 17:1; 26:37). John and James, his older brother, were known as "the sons of Zebedee," and Jesus called them "Sons of Thunder" (Matt. 10:2–4; Mark 3:17). After Christ's ascension, John became a pillar in the Jerusalem church.

He ministered with Peter until he went to Ephesus (tradition says before the destruction of Jerusalem), from where the Romans exiled him to Patmos. Besides the book of Revelation, John also authored the Gospel that bears his name, as well as 1 John, 2 John, and 3 John.

## UNLEASHING THE TEXT

Read 1:1–20, noting the key words and definitions next to the passage.

### Revelation 1:1–20 (NKJV)

1 *The Revelation of Jesus Christ, which God gave Him to show His servants—things which must shortly take place. And He sent and signified it by His angel to His servant John,*

2 *who bore witness to the word of God, and to the testimony of Jesus Christ, to all things that he saw.*

3 *Blessed is he who reads and those who hear the words of this prophecy, and keep those things which are written in it; for the time is near.*

4 *John, to the seven churches which are in Asia: Grace to you and peace from Him who is and who was and who is to come, and from the seven Spirits who are before His throne,*

5 *and from Jesus Christ, the faithful witness, the firstborn from the dead, and the ruler over the kings of the earth. To Him who loved us and washed us from our sins in His own blood,*

**Jesus Christ** (v. 1)—The Gospels unveil Christ's coming in humiliation; the book of Revelation reveals Him in His exaltation.

**God gave Him** (v. 1)—As a reward for Christ's perfect submission and atonement, the Father now presented to Him the great record of His future glory.

**shortly** (v. 1)—The primary meaning of this word (literally "soon"; see 2:5, 16; 3:11; 11:14; 22:12) underscores the imminence of Christ's return.

**Blessed** (v. 3)—This is the only biblical book that comes with a blessing for the one who listens to its message and then responds in obedience. This is the first of seven beatitudes in the book (v. 3; 14:13; 16:15; 19:9; 20:6; 22:7, 14).

**time is near** (v. 3)—"Time" refers to epochs, eras, or seasons. The next great epoch of God's redemptive history is imminent. But although Christ's coming is the next event, it may be delayed so long that people begin to question whether He will ever come.

**seven churches which are in Asia** (v. 4)—Asia Minor, equivalent to modern Turkey, was composed of seven administrative districts. At the center of those districts were seven key cities which served as central points for the dissemination of information. It is to the churches in those cities that John writes.

**who is and who was and who is to come** (v. 4)—God's eternal presence is not limited by time. He has always been present and will come in the future.

**the seven Spirits** (v. 4)—There are two possible meanings: (1) a reference to Isaiah's prophecy concerning the sevenfold ministry of the Holy Spirit (Isa. 11:2); or (2) more likely, it is a reference to the lampstand with seven lamps (a menorah) in Zechariah—also a description of the Holy Spirit. In either case, seven is the number of completeness, so John is identifying the fullness of the Holy Spirit.

**firstborn** (v. 5)—Of all who have been or will be raised from the dead, Jesus is the preeminent One, the only One who is the rightful heir (see 3:14).

**kings and priests** (v. 6)—This would be translated more accurately, "a kingdom and priests." All who believe live in the sphere of God's rule, a kingdom entered by faith in Jesus Christ. And as priests, believers have the right to enter God's presence.

**coming with clouds** (v. 7)—This echoes the promise of Daniel: The Son of Man will come with the clouds of heaven (Dan. 7:13)—not ordinary clouds but clouds of glory. In the Old Testament, God often manifested Himself in an energized, blazing light, called the Shekinah or glory cloud. No one could see it fully and live (Exod. 33:20), so it had to be veiled. But when Christ returns, the glory will be completely visible.

**they who pierced** (v. 7)—This is not a reference to the four Roman soldiers usually involved in Christ's crucifixion, but to the Jews who were actually responsible for Christ's death (Acts 2:22–23; 3:14–15). Zechariah identified the ones who pierced Him as "the house of David" and "the inhabitants of Jerusalem," and prophesied that they will weep tears of genuine repentance because of what they did to their Messiah.

**all the tribes . . . will mourn** (v. 7)—The mourning of the rest of the earth's inhabitants is not that which accompanies genuine repentance (see 9:21). It is the result of guilt for sin and fear of punishment.

**Alpha and the Omega** (v. 8)—These are the first and last letters of the Greek alphabet. An alphabet is an ingenious way to store and communicate knowledge. The twenty-six letters in the English alphabet, arranged in almost endless combinations, can hold and convey all knowledge. Christ is the supreme, sovereign alphabet; there is nothing outside His knowledge, so there are no unknown factors that can sabotage His second coming (see Col. 2:3).

**the Almighty** (v. 8)—"Almighty God" occurs eight times in Revelation, underscoring that God's power is supreme over all the cataclysmic events it records (see also 4:8; 11:17; 15:3; 16:7, 14; 19:15; 21:22). He exercises sovereign control over every person, object, and event, and not one molecule in the universe is outside that dominion.

**tribulation and kingdom and patience** (v. 9)—Four characteristics that John and his believing readers share are: (1) persecution for their faith; (2) membership in the redeemed community over which Christ serves as Lord and King; (3) eager anticipation of the glory of His coming millennial reign on earth; and (4) endurance and perseverance in spite of difficult times.

**island . . . called Patmos** (v. 9)—Located in the Aegean Sea off the coast of Asia Minor (modern Turkey) and part of a group of about fifty islands, Patmos is a barren, rocky, crescent-shaped island that is about ten miles long and less than six miles at its widest point. It served as a Roman penal colony. According to the early Christian historian Eusebius, the emperor Nerva (AD 96–98) released John from Patmos.

**in the Spirit** (v. 10)—This was not a dream. John was supernaturally transported out of the material world while awake—not sleeping—to an experience beyond the normal senses. The Holy Spirit empowered his senses to perceive revelation from God.

6 and has made us kings and priests to His God and Father, to Him be glory and dominion forever and ever. Amen.

7 Behold, He is coming with clouds, and every eye will see Him, even they who pierced Him. And all the tribes of the earth will mourn because of Him. Even so, Amen.

8 "I am the Alpha and the Omega, the Beginning and the End," says the Lord, "who is and who was and who is to come, the Almighty."

9 I, John, both your brother and companion in the tribulation and kingdom and patience of Jesus Christ, was on the island that is called Patmos for the word of God and for the testimony of Jesus Christ.

10 I was in the Spirit on the Lord's Day, and I heard behind me a loud voice, as of a trumpet,

11 saying, "I am the Alpha and the Omega, the First and the Last," and, "What you see, write in a book and send it to the seven churches which are in Asia: to Ephesus, to Smyrna, to Pergamos, to Thyatira, to Sardis, to Philadelphia, and to Laodicea."

12 Then I turned to see the voice that spoke with me. And having turned I saw seven golden lampstands,

13 and in the midst of the seven lampstands One like the Son of Man, clothed with a garment down to the feet and girded about the chest with a golden band.

14 His head and hair were white like wool, as white as snow, and His eyes like a flame of fire;

15 His feet were like fine brass, as if refined in a furnace, and His voice as the sound of many waters;

16 He had in His right hand seven stars, out of His mouth went a sharp two-edged sword, and His countenance was like the sun shining in its strength.

**Lord's Day** (v. 10)—This phrase appears in many early Christian writings and refers to Sunday, the day of the Lord's resurrection. Some have suggested this phrase refers to "the Day of the Lord," but the context doesn't support that interpretation, and the grammatical form of the word "Lord" is adjectival, thus "the Lord's day."

**loud voice** (v. 10)—Throughout Revelation, a loud sound or voice indicates the solemnity of what God is about to reveal.

**book** (v. 11)—The Greek word refers to a scroll made of parchment formed from papyrus, a reed that grows plentifully along the Nile.

**lampstands** (v. 12)—These were portable gold lampstands that held small oil lamps. Each lampstand represented a church (v. 20), from which the light of life shone. Throughout Scripture, seven is the number of completeness, so these seven lampstands are representative of all the churches.

**Son of Man** (v. 13)—According to the Gospels, this is the title Christ used most often for Himself during His earthly ministry (eighty-one times in the Gospels). Taken from the heavenly vision in Daniel 7:13, it is an implied claim to deity.

**garment** (v. 13)—Most occurrences of this word in the Septuagint, the Greek Old Testament, refer to the garment of the high priest. The golden sash across His chest completes the picture of Christ serving in His priestly role.

**white like wool** (v. 14)—"White" does not refer to a flat white color but to a blazing, glowing, white light symbolizing holiness.

**eyes . . . flame of fire** (v. 14)—Like two lasers, the eyes of the exalted Lord look with a penetrating gaze into the depths of His church (2:18; 19:12).

**feet . . . fine brass** (v. 15)—The altar of burnt offering was covered with brass and its utensils were made of the same material (see Exod. 38:1–7). Glowing hot, brass feet are a clear reference to divine judgment. Jesus Christ with feet of judgment is moving through His church to exercise His chastening authority upon sin.

**Voice . . . sound of many waters** (v. 15)—No longer was His voice like the clear note of a trumpet (v. 10), but John likened it to the crashing of the surf against the rocks of the island. It was the voice of authority.

**seven stars** (v. 16)—These are the messengers who represent the seven churches (see the note on v. 20). Christ holds them in His hand, which means that He controls the church and its leaders.

**a sharp two-edged sword** (v. 16)—The large, two-edged broad sword signifies judgment (see 2:16; 19:15) on those who attack His people and destroy His church.

*fell at His feet* (v. 17)—a common response to seeing the awesome glory of the Lord

*First and the Last* (v. 17)—Jesus Christ applies this Old Testament name for Yahweh (see 22:13) to Himself, clearly claiming to be God. Idols will come and go. He was before them, and He will remain after them.

*keys of Hades and of Death* (v. 18)—Death and Hades are essentially synonyms, but death is the condition and Hades, equivalent to the Old Testament Sheol, the place of the dead. Christ decides who lives, who dies, and when.

17 *And when I saw Him, I fell at His feet as dead. But He laid His right hand on me, saying to me, "Do not be afraid; I am the First and the Last.*

18 *I am He who lives, and was dead, and behold, I am alive forevermore. Amen. And I have the keys of Hades and of Death.*

19 *Write the things which you have seen, and the things which are, and the things which will take place after this.*

20 *The mystery of the seven stars which you saw in My right hand, and the seven golden lampstands: The seven stars are the angels of the seven churches, and the seven lampstands which you saw are the seven churches."*

*the angels* (v. 20)—The word literally means "messenger." Although it can mean angel—and does throughout the book—it cannot refer to angels here because angels are never leaders in the church. Most likely, these messengers are the seven key elders representing each of those churches.

1) What did John mean when he wrote "the time is near"?

_____

_____

_____

_____

_____

_____

*(Verses to consider: Matt. 24:36–39; 2 Pet. 3:3–4)*

2) How did John describe the future second coming of Christ?

_____

_____

_____

_____

_____

_____

3) How will unbelievers (Jews and Gentiles) respond to the return of Christ?

_____

_____

_____

_____

*(Verse to consider: Zech. 12:10)*

4) Describe the amazing appearance of the Son of Man in this vision (vv. 13–18). What do these images convey about Christ?

_____

_____

_____

_____

5) What effect did this vision of the risen Christ have on John?

_____

_____

_____

_____

*(Verses to consider: Gen. 17:3; Num. 16:22; Isa. 6:1–8; Ezek. 1:28; Acts 9:4)*

6) Why is Revelation 1:19 such a significant verse in relation to our understanding of this book?

_____

_____

_____

_____

## GOING DEEPER

Revelation gives us a glimpse of who Jesus really is and the glory and power that are His. For more insight about Jesus, read Philippians 2:5–11.

5 *Let this mind be in you which was also in Christ Jesus,*

6 *who, being in the form of God, did not consider it robbery to be equal with God,*

7 *but made Himself of no reputation, taking the form of a bondservant, and coming in the likeness of men.*

8 *And being found in appearance as a man, He humbled Himself and became obedient to the point of death, even the death of the cross.*

9 *Therefore God also has highly exalted Him and given Him the name which is above every name,*

10 *that at the name of Jesus every knee should bow, of those in heaven, and of those on earth, and of those under the earth,*

11 *and that every tongue should confess that Jesus Christ is Lord, to the glory of God the Father.*

## EXPLORING THE MEANING

7) What do you learn here about Jesus' identity? How is this identity affirmed in Revelation 1?

_____

_____

_____

_____

_____

8) What does Philippians 2 say about Christ's past humiliation and its relationship to His present and future exaltation?

_____

_____

_____

_____

_____

9) Read Matthew 24:29–30 and 25:31. What do these passages add to your understanding of the second coming of Christ?

_____

_____

_____

_____

_____

10) Read John 11:25 and 14:6. What do these verses say about Christ being "He who lives" (Rev. 1:18)?

_____

_____

_____

_____

_____

*(Verses to consider: Rom. 6:9; Heb. 2:14–15; 7:16; 1 Pet. 3:18)*

## TRUTH FOR TODAY

Jesus came the first time in humiliation; He will return in exaltation. He came the first time to die; He will return to judge His enemies. He came the first time to serve; He will return to be served. He came the first time as the suffering servant; He will return as the conquering king. The challenge the book of Revelation makes to every person is to be ready for His return.

## REFLECTING ON THE TEXT

11) Imagine seeing a vision such as John saw. When in your life have you had a profound experience or encounter with the living God? What happened? How were you affected?

_____

_____

_____

_____

12) What does it mean to you that Christ, the Alpha and Omega, the King of kings, loves you and washed away your sins with His blood (v. 2)?

_____

_____

_____

_____

_____

13) How would your life be different (practically and specifically) if you lived each day with a continual expectancy of Christ's return?

_____

_____

_____

_____

_____

## PERSONAL RESPONSE

Write out additional reflections, questions you may have, or a prayer.

_____

_____

_____

_____

_____

_____

_____

_____

_____

_____

# 2

# MESSAGE TO THE CHURCHES, PART 1
*Revelation 2:1–29*

## DRAWING NEAR

In the vision, Jesus instructs John to write letters to various churches. If Jesus were to send a message to your local church, what things might He commend your church for? Rebuke you for? Why do you think so?

_____

_____

_____

_____

How would you define the term "Christian"?

_____

_____

_____

_____

## THE CONTEXT

In his book *The Mark of the Christian,* theologian Francis Schaeffer once observed, "The meaning of the word *Christian* has been reduced to practically nothing . . . Because the word *Christian* as a symbol has been made to mean so little, it has come to mean everything and nothing." The term *Christian* in contemporary usage can mean anyone who is not Jewish, anyone who lives in a "Christian" nation (as opposed, for example, to a Buddhist or an Islamic one), or anyone who claims any kind of allegiance to Jesus Christ. Though the world may be confused about what a Christian is, the Bible is clear. Christians are those who are united to God through saving faith in Jesus Christ and thus are members of His body, the church.

The seven churches addressed in chapters 2 and 3 were real churches when John lived. Five of the seven churches were rebuked for tolerating sin in their midst, not an uncommon occurrence in many churches. The problems in those churches ranged in severity from waning love at Ephesus to total apostasy at Laodicea. They weren't living like real Christians should. It is important for readers to understand that any church in any age can have a mixture of the sins that plagued these five churches . . . or it can persevere and be commended as were the churches at Smyrna and Philadelphia.

## KEYS TO THE TEXT

*The Church:* God's people, the universal body of believers as well as the local group of believers. The church is the "body of Christ" (Rom. 12:5). This metaphor depicts the church not as an organization but as a living organism composed of mutually related and interdependent parts. Christ is Head of the body and the Holy Spirit is its lifeblood, as it were. The body functions through the faithful use of its members' various spiritual gifts, sovereignly and uniquely bestowed by the Holy Spirit on each believer. Because Christians are part of the body of Christ, have been spiritually gifted by the Holy Spirit, and are edified through other believers, they should not continue to live like the ungodly.

## UNLEASHING THE TEXT

Read 2:1–29, noting the key words and definitions next to the passage.

### Revelation 2:1–29 (NKJV)

*angel* (v. 1)—the elder or pastor from the church

*Ephesus* (v. 1)—This was an inland city three miles from the sea, but the broad mouth of the Cayster River allowed access and provided the greatest harbor in Asia Minor. Four great trade roads went through Ephesus; therefore, it became known as the gateway to Asia. It was the center of the worship of Artemis (Greek), or Diana (Roman), whose temple was one of the Seven Wonders of the Ancient World. Paul minis-

1 "To the angel of the church of Ephesus write, 'These things says He who holds the seven stars in His right hand, who walks in the midst of the seven golden lampstands:

2 "I know your works, your labor, your patience, and that you cannot bear those who are evil. And you have tested those who say they are apostles and are not, and have found them liars;

3 and you have persevered and have patience, and have labored for My name's sake and have not become weary.

tered there for three years (Acts 20:31) and later met with the Ephesian elders on his way to Jerusalem (Acts 20). Timothy, Tychicus, and the apostle John all served this church; John was in Ephesus when he was arrested by Domitian and exiled fifty miles southwest to Patmos.

*who say they are apostles* (v. 2)—The Ephesian church exercised spiritual discernment. It knew how to evaluate men who claimed spiritual leadership, judging them by their doctrine and behavior.

*not become weary* (v. 3)—For over forty years, since its founding, this church had remained faithful to the Word and the Lord. Through difficulty and persecution, the members had endured, always driven by the right motive, that is, Christ's name and reputation.

4 *Nevertheless I have this against you, that you have left your first love.*

5 *Remember therefore from where you have fallen; repent and do the first works, or else I will come to you quickly and remove your lampstand from its place—unless you repent.*

6 *But this you have, that you hate the deeds of the Nicolaitans, which I also hate.*

7 *"He who has an ear, let him hear what the Spirit says to the churches. To him who overcomes I will give to eat from the tree of life, which is in the midst of the Paradise of God." '*

8 *"And to the angel of the church in Smyrna write, 'These things says the First and the Last, who was dead, and came to life:*

9 *"I know your works, tribulation, and poverty (but you are rich); and I know the blasphemy of those who say they are Jews and are not, but are a synagogue of Satan.*

10 *Do not fear any of those things which you are about to suffer. Indeed, the devil is about to throw some*

**left your first love** (v. 4)—To be a Christian is to love the Lord Jesus Christ. But the Ephesians' passion and fervor for Christ had become cold, mechanical orthodoxy. Their doctrinal and moral purity, their undiminished zeal for the truth, and their disciplined service were no substitute for the love for Christ they had forsaken.

**remove your lampstand** (v. 5)—God's judgment would bring an end to the Ephesian church.

**the deeds of the Nicolaitans** (v. 6)—A problem in Pergamos also (vv. 12–15), this heresy was similar to the teaching of Balaam (vv. 14–15). Nicolas means "one who conquers the people." Irenaeus writes that Nicolas, who was made a deacon in Acts 6, was a false believer who later became apostate. Because of his credentials he was able to lead the church astray, and, like Balaam, he led the people into immorality and wickedness. The Nicolaitans, followers of Nicolas, were involved in immorality and assaulted the church with sensual temptations. Clement of Alexander says, "They abandoned themselves to pleasure like goats, leading a life of self-indulgence." Their teaching perverted grace and replaced liberty with license.

**him who overcomes** (v. 7)—According to John's own definition, to be an overcomer is to be a Christian (see vv. 11, 17, 26; 3:5, 12, 21).

**tree of life** (v. 7)—True believers enjoy the promise of heaven (see notes on 22:2; Gen. 2:9).

**Smyrna** (v. 8)—Smyrna means "myrrh," the substance used for perfume and often for anointing a dead body for aromatic purposes. Called the crown of Asia, this ancient city (modern Izmir, Turkey) was the most beautiful in Asia Minor and a center of science and medicine. Always on the winner's side in the Roman wars, Smyrna's intense loyalty to Rome resulted in a strong emperor-worship cult. Fifty years after John's death, Polycarp, the bishop or pastor of the church in Smyrna, was burned alive at the age of eighty-six for refusing to worship Caesar. A large Jewish community in the city also proved hostile to the early church.

**who say they are Jews** (v. 9)—Although they were Jews physically, they were not true Jews but spiritual pagans (see Rom. 2:28), who allied with other pagans in putting Christians to death as they attempted to stamp out the Christian faith.

**synagogue of Satan** (v. 9)—With the rejection of its Messiah, Judaism becomes as much a tool of Satan as emperor worship.

**devil** (v. 10)—The Greek name for God's archenemy means "accuser."

**tribulation ten days** (v. 10)—Their imprisonment will be brief.

**crown of life** (v. 10)—It is the crown which is life, or the reward which is life, not an actual crown to adorn the head. "Crown" here does not refer to the kind royalty wear, but to the wreath awarded to winning athletes.

**who overcomes** (v. 11)—This identifies every Christian (see note on v. 7).

**the second death** (v. 11)—The first death is only physical; the second is spiritual and eternal (see 20:14).

**Pergamos** (v. 12)—Pergamos literally means "citadel" and is the word from which we get "parchment"—a writing material developed from animal skin, which apparently was first developed in that area. Pergamos (modern Bergama) was built on a thousand-foot hill in a broad, fertile plain about twenty miles inland from the Aegean Sea. It

of you into prison, that you may be tested, and you will have tribulation ten days. Be faithful until death, and I will give you the crown of life.

11 "He who has an ear, let him hear what the Spirit says to the churches. He who overcomes shall not be hurt by the second death." '

12 "And to the angel of the church in Pergamos write, 'These things says He who has the sharp two-edged sword:

13 "I know your works, and where you dwell, where Satan's throne is. And you hold fast to My name, and did not deny My faith even in the days in which Antipas was My faithful martyr, who was killed among you, where Satan dwells.

14 But I have a few things against you, because you have there those who hold the doctrine of Balaam, who taught Balak to put a stumbling block before the children of Israel, to eat things sacrificed to idols, and to commit sexual immorality.

15 Thus you also have those who hold the doctrine of the Nicolaitans, which thing I hate.

had served as the capital of the Roman province of Asia Minor for over two hundred fifty years. It was an important religious center for the pagan cults of Athena, Asklepios, Dionysus (or Bacchus, the god of drunkenness), and Zeus. It was the first city in Asia to build a temple to Caesar (29 BC) and became the capital of the cult of Caesar worship.

**where Satan's throne is** (v. 13)—This was the headquarters of satanic opposition and a Gentile base for false religions. On the acropolis in Pergamos was a huge, throne-shaped altar to Zeus. In addition, Asklepios, the god of healing, was the god most associated with Pergamos. His snake-like form is still the medical symbol today. The famous medical school connected to his temple mingled medicine with superstition. One prescription called for the worshiper to sleep on the temple floor, allowing snakes to crawl over his body and infuse him with their healing power.

**Antipas** (v. 13)—probably the pastor of the church

**faithful martyr** (v. 13)—Tradition says Antipas was burned to death inside a brass bull. Martyr, a transliteration of the Greek word, means "witness." Because so many of the witnesses faithful to Christ were put to death, the word martyr developed its current definition.

**doctrine of Balaam** (v. 14)—Balaam tried unsuccessfully to prostitute his prophetic gift and curse Israel for money offered him by Balak, king of Moab. So he devised a plot to have Moabite women seduce Israelite men into intermarriage. The result was the blasphemous union of Israel with fornication and idolatrous feasts (for the story of Balaam, see Num. 22–25).

**Thus you also** (v. 15)—The teaching of the Nicolaitans led to the same behavior as Balaam's schemes.

**hidden manna** (v. 17)—Just as Israel received manna, God promises to give the true believer the spiritual bread the unbelieving world cannot see: Jesus Christ (see John 6:51).

16 *Repent, or else I will come to you quickly and will fight against them with the sword of My mouth.*

17 *"He who has an ear, let him hear what the Spirit says to the churches. To him who overcomes I will give some of the hidden manna to eat. And I will give him a white stone, and on the stone a new name written which no one knows except him who receives it." '*

18 *"And to the angel of the church in Thyatira write, 'These things says the Son of God, who has eyes like a flame of fire, and His feet like fine brass:*

19 *"I know your works, love, service, faith, and your patience; and as for your works, the last are more than the first.*

20 *Nevertheless I have a few things against you, because you allow that woman Jezebel, who calls herself a prophetess, to teach and seduce My servants to commit sexual immorality and eat things sacrificed to idols.*

21 *And I gave her time to repent of her sexual immorality, and she did not repent.*

22 *Indeed I will cast her into a sickbed, and those who commit adultery with her into great tribulation, unless they repent of their deeds.*

23 *I will kill her children with death, and all the churches shall know that I am He who searches the minds and hearts. And I will give to each one of you according to your works.*

**white stone** (v. 17)—When an athlete won in the games, he was often given as part of his prize a white stone, which was an admission pass to the winner's celebration afterwards. This may depict the moment when the overcomer will receive his ticket to the eternal victory celebration in heaven.

**new name** (v. 17)—A personal message from Christ to the ones He loves, which serves as their admission pass into eternal glory. It is so personal that only the person who receives it will know what it is.

**Thyatira** (v. 18)—Located halfway between Pergamos and Sardis, this city had been under Roman rule for nearly three centuries (about 190 BC). Since the city was situated in a long valley that swept forty miles to Pergamos, it had no natural defenses and had a long history of being destroyed and rebuilt. Originally populated by soldiers of Alexander the Great, it was little more than a military outpost to guard Pergamos. Lydia came from this city on business and was converted under Paul's ministry (Acts 16:14–15).

**Jezebel** (v. 20)—Probably a pseudonym for a woman who influenced the church in the way Jezebel influenced the Old Testament Jews into idolatry and immorality (see 1 Kings 21:25–26).

**sickbed** (v. 22)—This is literally "bed." Having given this woman time to repent, God was to judge her upon a bed. Since she used a luxurious bed to commit her immorality, and the reclining couch at the idol feast to eat things offered to false gods, He was to give her a bed in hell where she would lie forever.

**her children** (v. 23)—The church was about forty years old as John wrote this book, and her teaching had produced a second generation, advocating the same debauchery.

**who searches the minds and hearts.** (v. 23)—God has perfect, intimate knowledge of every human heart; no evil can be hidden from Him (Ps. 7:9; Prov. 24:12; Jer. 11:20; 17:10; 20:12).

**according to your works** (v. 23)—Works do not save (Eph. 2:8–9), however, they do evidence salvation (James 2:14–26), and we will be judged in the future by them (20:12–13; Matt. 16:27; Rom. 2:6).

**the depths of Satan** (v. 24)—This unbelievable libertinism and license was the fruit of pre-gnostic teaching, saying that one was free to engage and explore the sphere of Satan and participate in evil with the body without harming the spirit.

**rule them with a rod of iron** (v. 27)—literally "shepherd them with an iron rod." During the millennial kingdom, Christ will enforce His will and protect his sheep with His iron scepter from any who would seek to harm them (see Ps. 2:9).

**the morning star** (v. 28)—John later reveals Christ to be "the morning star." Although the morning star has already dawned in our hearts (2 Pet. 1:19), someday we will have Him in His fullness.

24 *"Now to you I say, and to the rest in Thyatira, as many as do not have this doctrine, who have not known the depths of Satan, as they say, I will put on you no other burden.*

25 *But hold fast what you have till I come.*

26 *And he who overcomes, and keeps My works until the end, to him I will give power over the nations—*

27 *'He shall rule them with a rod of iron; They shall be dashed to pieces like the potter's vessels'— as I also have received from My Father;*

28 *and I will give him the morning star.*

29 *"He who has an ear, let him hear what the Spirit says to the churches." ' "*

1) What commendations did Christ have for the church at Ephesus? For what sin did he rebuke them?

_____

_____

_____

_____

*(Verses to consider: Acts 18:19–21; 19:1–35; 20:17–38)*

2) What situation did the church at Smyrna face? What did God promise them? How do these facts square with the expectations of most Western Christians?

_____

_____

_____

_____

*(Verses to consider: Acts 14:22; 2 Tim. 3:12; James 1:2–4; 1 Pet. 5:10)*

3) What was the great sin of the church of Pergamos?

_____

_____

_____

_____

4) Summarize Christ's message for the church at Thyatira.

_____

_____

_____

5) Note the varied descriptions Jesus gives of Himself (vv. 1, 8, 12, 18). What do these reveal about Him?

_____

_____

_____

_____

6) Review Jesus' commands to each church (vv. 5, 10, 16, 25). How do Jesus' commands fit the problem He exposed in each church?

_____

_____

_____

_____

## GOING DEEPER

Unfaithfulness and hypocrisy among God's people is nothing new. For more insight about how the world can affect the church, read 1 John 2:15–17.

> 15 *Do not love the world or the things in the world. If anyone loves the world, the love of the Father is not in him.*
> 16 *For all that is in the world—the lust of the flesh, the lust of the eyes, and the pride of life—is not of the Father but is of the world.*
> 17 *And the world is passing away, and the lust of it; but he who does the will of God abides forever.*

## Exploring the Meaning

7) How is the world system defined in this passage? What does it mean to love the world?

_____

_____

_____

_____

8) What antidote does 1 John 2 provide to guard against being led astray, like the church of Pergamos was?

_____

_____

_____

_____

9) Read Matthew 18:15–17. Why is it so important for the church to address sin in its midst? What is the right way to do this, according to Christ's teaching?

_____

_____

_____

_____

## Truth for Today

For many people in today's church, the term _worldliness_ has a quaint, old-fashioned ring to it. They associate it with prohibitions against things like dancing, going to the movies, or playing cards. Today's user-friendly, seeker-oriented, market-driven church doesn't preach much against worldliness. To do so might make unbelievers (not to mention many believers) uncomfortable, and is therefore avoided as poor marketing strategy. But unlike much of the contemporary church, the Bible does not hesitate to condemn worldliness for the serious sin that it is. Worldliness is any preoccupation with or interest in the temporal system of life that places anything perishable before that which is eternal.

## REFLECTING ON THE TEXT

10) How has this passage added to or changed your view of what a real "Christian" is?

_____

_____

_____

_____

11) What worldly attitudes or actions do you find yourself struggling with the most? What principles from Revelation 2:12–17 offer you hope for change?

_____

_____

_____

_____

12) What counsel would you give to a Christian friend who confessed that he or she had lost their "first love" for Christ?

_____

_____

_____

_____

13) Jesus urged, "He who has an ear, let him hear what the Spirit says." What keeps you from hearing God's voice? Ask Him to help you slow down and learn how to hear Him, and then obey.

_____

_____

_____

_____

## PERSONAL RESPONSE

Write out additional reflections, questions you may have, or a prayer.

# 3

# MESSAGE TO THE CHURCHES, PART 2
## *Revelation 3:1–22*

## DRAWING NEAR

Jesus challenged these seven ancient churches to stay faithful. What have you learned thus far about what is essential for a vibrant, healthy church?

_____

_____

_____

_____

## THE CONTEXT

This passage continues the series of Jesus' messages to the churches of Sardis, Philadelphia, and Laodicea. The church at Sardis was an existing church in John's day but spiritually it had no life. It stands as a symbol of all dead churches. The church in Philadelphia had its imperfections, yet the Lord commended its members for their faithfulness and loyalty. In spite of their fleshly struggles, the Christians at Philadelphia were faithful and obedient, serving and worshiping the Lord. They provide a good model of a loyal church. The last church addressed by Jesus was at Laodicea, and it represents all the apostate churches that have existed throughout history. Laodicea has the grim distinction of being the only one of the seven for whom Christ has no positive word of commendation. Due to the drastic nature of the situation at Laodicea, this is also the most threatening of the seven letters.

## KEYS TO THE TEXT

*Book of Life:* This is the first mention of this divine journal. This book records the names of all those whom God has chosen to save and who, therefore, are to possess eternal life (13:8; 17:8; 20:12, 15; 21:27; 22:19). Under no circumstances will God erase those names, as city officials often did of undesirable people on their rolls.

*Jesus Christ:* Revelation makes it clear that Jesus is the "Alpha and Omega", the "Beginning and the End." He is the "Beginning" (literally "beginner, originator, initiator") of creation and the "firstborn of creation"; that is, the most preeminent, supreme person ever born (Col. 1:15). As a man, he had a beginning; but as God, He was the beginning. Sadly, in Laodicea the heresy that Christ was just a created being had produced an unregenerate church.

## UNLEASHING THE TEXT

Read 3:1–22, noting the key words and definitions next to the passage.

### Revelation 3:1–22 (NKJV)

*angel* (v. 1)—messenger or pastor

*Sardis* (v. 1)—Situated on a natural acropolis rising fifteen hundred feet above the valley floor, the city (modern Sart) was nearly impregnable. Around 1200 BC it gained prominence as the capital of the Lydian kingdom. Its primary industry was harvesting wool, dying it, and making garments from it. The famous author Aesop came from Sardis, and tradition says that Mileto, a member of the church in Sardis, wrote the first-ever commentary on certain passages in the book of Revelation. But the church in Sardis was dead; that is, it was basically populated by unredeemed, unregenerate people.

*seven stars* (v. 1)—the pastors of these seven churches

*come upon you as a thief* (v. 3)—Here the reference is not to Christ's second coming (see 16:1), but to His sudden and unexpected coming to His unrepentant, dead church to inflict harm and destruction.

1 *"And to the angel of the church in Sardis write,*
*'These things says He who has the seven Spirits of*
*God and the seven stars: "I know your works, that*
*you have a name that you are alive, but you are*
*dead.*

2 *Be watchful, and strengthen the things which*
*remain, that are ready to die, for I have not found*
*your works perfect before God.*

3 *Remember therefore how you have received and*
*heard; hold fast and repent. Therefore if you will not*
*watch, I will come upon you as a thief, and you will*
*not know what hour I will come upon you.*

4 *You have a few names even in Sardis who have not*
*defiled their garments; and they shall walk with Me*
*in white, for they are worthy.*

5 *He who overcomes shall be clothed in white*
*garments, and I will not blot out his name from the*
*Book of Life; but I will confess his name before My*
*Father and before His angels.*

6 *"He who has an ear, let him hear what the Spirit*
*says to the churches." '*

*who have not defiled their garments* (v. 4)—Defiled means "smeared, polluted," or "stained," and garments refers to character. There were a few whose character was still godly (see Jude 23).

*in white* (v. 4)—The white garments of all the redeemed (see 6:11; 7:9, 13; 19:8, 14) speak of holiness and purity. Such white robes are reserved for Christ (Matt. 17:2), holy angels (Matt. 28:3), and the glorified church (19:8, 14). In the ancient world, white robes were commonly worn at festivals and celebrations.

*overcomes* (v. 5)—all true Christians

7 "And to the angel of the church in Philadelphia write, 'These things says He who is holy, He who is true, "He who has the key of David, He who opens and no one shuts, and shuts and no one opens"':

8 "I know your works. See, I have set before you an open door, and no one can shut it; for you have a little strength, have kept My word, and have not denied My name.

9 Indeed I will make those of the synagogue of Satan, who say they are Jews and are not, but lie—indeed I will make them come and worship before your feet, and to know that I have loved you.

10 Because you have kept My command to persevere, I also will keep you from the hour of trial which shall come upon the whole world, to test those who dwell on the earth.

11 Behold, I am coming quickly! Hold fast what you have, that no one may take your crown.

12 He who overcomes, I will make him a pillar in the temple of My God, and he shall go out no more. I will write on him the name of My God and the name of the city of My God, the New Jerusalem,

**Philadelphia** (v. 7)—Located on a hillside about thirty miles southeast of Sardis, the city (modern Alashehir) was founded around 190 BC by Attalus II, king of Pergamos. His unusual devotion to his brother earned the city its name, "brotherly love." The city was an important commercial stop on a major trade route called the Imperial Post Road, a first-century mail route. Although Scripture does not mention this church elsewhere, it was probably the fruit of Paul's extended ministry in Ephesus (see Acts 19:10).

**holy . . . true** (v. 7)—This is a common description in this book (4:8; 6:10; 15:3; 16:7; 19:2, 11). Christ shares the holy, sinless, pure nature of His Father (Ps. 16:10; Isa. 6:3; Hab. 3:3; Mark 1:11; John 6:69); that is, He is absolutely pure and separate from sin. "True" can refer both to one who speaks truth and to one who is genuine or authentic as opposed to fake.

**the key of David** (v. 7)—Christ has the sovereign authority to control entrance into the kingdom (Isa. 22:22; see Matt. 16:19). In 1:18 He is pictured holding the keys to death and hell; here he holds the keys to salvation and blessing.

**open door** (v. 8)—This is either admission into the kingdom (see v. 7) or an opportunity for service.

**keep you from the hour of trial** (v. 10)—Christ's description of a future event that for a short time severely tests the whole world must refer to the time of tribulation, the seven-year period before Christ's earthly kingdom is consummated, featuring the unleashing of divine wrath in judgments expressed as seals, trumpets, and bowls. This period is described in detail throughout chapters 6–19. The latter half of this time period is called "the Great Tribulation" (7:14; Matt. 24:21). The verb "to keep" is followed by a preposition whose normal meaning is "from" or "out of"—this phrase, "keep . . . from" supports the pretribulational rapture of the church.

**I am coming quickly!** (v. 11)—This isn't the threatening temporal judgment described in verse 3; 2:5, 16, nor the final judgment of chapter 19; it is a hopeful event. Christ will return to take His church out of the hour of trial.

**He who overcomes** (v. 12)—all Christians

**a pillar** (v. 12)—Believers will enjoy an unshakable, eternal, secure place in the presence of God.

**write . . . name of My God** (v. 12)—In biblical times, one's name spoke of a person's character. Writing His name on us speaks of imprinting His character on us and identifying us as belonging to Him.

**New Jerusalem** (v. 12)—the capital city of heaven (see 21:1–27). The overcomer will enjoy eternal citizenship.

**My new name** (v. 12)—At the moment we see Christ, whatever we may have called Him and understood by that name will pale in the reality of what we see. And He will give us a new, eternal name by which we will know Him.

**angel** (v. 14)—the pastor-messenger designated to deliver this letter

**Laodiceans** (v. 14)—Located in the Lycus River Valley, the southwest area of Phrygia, Laodicea became the wealthiest, most important commercial center in the region. It was primarily known for three industries: banking, wool, and medicine (notably its eye salve). An inadequate local water supply forced the city to build an under-ground aqueduct. All three industries, as well as the inadequate water supply, played a major part in this letter. The church began through the ministry of Epaphras, while Paul was ministering in Ephesus (see Col. 1:7; Paul never personally visited Laodicea).

which comes down out of heaven from My God. And I will write on him My new name.

13 "He who has an ear, let him hear what the Spirit says to the churches." '

14 "And to the angel of the church of the Laodiceans write, 'These things says the Amen, the Faithful and True Witness, the Beginning of the creation of God:

15 "I know your works, that you are neither cold nor hot. I could wish you were cold or hot.

16 So then, because you are lukewarm, and neither cold nor hot, I will vomit you out of My mouth.

17 Because you say, 'I am rich, have become wealthy, and have need of nothing'—and do not know that you are wretched, miserable, poor, blind, and naked—

18 I counsel you to buy from Me gold refined in the fire, that you may be rich; and white garments, that you may be clothed, that the shame of your nakedness may not be revealed; and anoint your eyes with eye salve, that you may see.

19 As many as I love, I rebuke and chasten. Therefore be zealous and repent.

**the Amen** (v. 14)—This is a common biblical expression signifying certainty and veracity (see Isa. 65:16, "the God of truth"). According to 2 Corinthians 1:20, all the promises of God are fulfilled in Christ; that is, all God's promises and unconditional covenants are guaranteed and affirmed by the person and work of Jesus Christ.

**Faithful and True Witness** (v. 14)—He is a completely trustworthy and perfectly accurate witness to the truth of God.

**Beginning of the creation** (v. 14)—This corrects a heresy, apparently present in Laodicea and in Colosse, that Christ was a created being.

**lukewarm** (v. 16)—Put another way, they were tepid. Nearby Hierapolis was famous for its hot springs, and Colosse for its cold, refreshing mountain stream. But Laodicea had dirty, tepid water that flowed for miles through an underground aqueduct. Visitors, unaccustomed to it, immediately spat it out. The church at Laodicea was neither cold, openly rejecting Christ, nor hot, filled with spiritual zeal. Instead, its members were lukewarm—hypocrites professing to know Christ but not truly belonging to Him (see Matt. 7:21–23).

**I will vomit you out of My mouth** (v. 16)—Just like the dirty, tepid water of Laodicea, these self-deceived hypocrites sickened Christ.

**gold . . . white garments . . . eye salve** (v. 18)—He was offering them the spiritual counterparts to their three major industries. Each item was a way to refer to genuine salvation.

**As many as I love . . . chasten** (v. 19)—Both verses 18 and 20 indicate that Christ was speaking here to unbelievers. God certainly loves the unconverted (see John 3:16). And "chasten" (literally "reprove") often refers to God's convicting and punishing the unregenerate (Matt. 18:17; 1 Cor. 14:24).

20 *Behold, I stand at the door and knock. If anyone hears My voice and opens the door, I will come in to him and dine with him, and he with Me.*

21 *To him who overcomes I will grant to sit with Me on My throne, as I also overcame and sat down with My Father on His throne.*

22 *"He who has an ear, let him hear what the Spirit says to the churches." ' "*

**I stand at the door and knock** (v. 20)—Rather than allowing for the common interpretation of Christ's knocking on a person's heart, the context demands that Christ was seeking to enter this church that bore His name but lacked a single true believer. This poignant letter was His knocking. If one member would recognize his spiritual bankruptcy and respond in saving faith, He would enter the church.

**sit with Me on My throne** (v. 21)—A figurative expression meaning that we will share the privilege and authority that Christ enjoys as we reign with Him (1:6).

1) What was the gist of Christ's message to the church at Sardis?

_____

_____

_____

_____

2) According to this passage, what was true about the church at Philadelphia?

_____

_____

_____

_____

_____

3) What is the significance of the crown mentioned in 3:11?

_____

_____

_____

_____

_____

*(Verses to consider: 2 Tim. 4:8; James 1:12; 1 Pet. 5:4; Rev. 2:10)*

4) What is revealed here about the church at Laodicea? What was its heresy? (See study notes on v. 14)

_____

_____

_____

_____

*(Verse to consider: John 1:3)*

5) How does Jesus describe Himself in these messages? What do these things teach you about Him?

_____

_____

_____

_____

6) What rewards were promised to those who "overcome"?

_____

_____

_____

_____

## GOING DEEPER

Heresy about Christ had invaded the church at Laodicea. For more insight into who Christ is, read Colossians 1:15–20.

15 *He is the image of the invisible God, the firstborn over all creation.*

16 *For by Him all things were created that are in heaven and that are on earth, visible and invisible, whether thrones or dominions or principalities or powers. All things were created through Him and for Him.*

17 *And He is before all things, and in Him all things consist.*

18 *And He is the head of the body, the church, who is the beginning, the firstborn from the dead, that in all things He may have the preeminence.*

19 *For it pleased the Father that in Him all the fullness should dwell,*

20 *and by Him to reconcile all things to Himself, by Him, whether things on earth or things in heaven, having made peace through the blood of His cross.*

## Exploring the Meaning

7) List all the ways this passage affirms that Jesus is more than a created being.

_____

_____

_____

_____

8) Why is Jesus worthy to be the head of the church?

_____

_____

_____

9) Read Daniel 12:1. What is the meaning of the phrase the "Book of Life" (see Rev. 3:5)?

_____

_____

_____

_____

*(Verses to consider: Exod. 32:31–33; Ps. 69:28; 139:16; Luke 10:20; Phil. 4:3)*

10) Read John 14:1–3. What promises did Christ give His followers concerning the time of tribulation and wrath to come?

_____

_____

_____

## Truth for Today

Occasionally I am asked by young men seeking to pastor a church if I know of a church without any problems. My response to them is, "If I did, I wouldn't tell you; you'd go there and spoil it." The point is that there are no perfect churches. Churches struggle because all are made up of imperfect sinning people. The church is not a place for people with no weaknesses; it is a fellowship of those who are aware of their weaknesses and long for the strength and grace of God to fill their lives. It is a kind of hospital for those who know they are sick and needy.

## Reflecting on the Text

11) Regarding the letter to the church at Laodicea, John R.W. Stott has written: "Perhaps none of the seven letters is more appropriate to the twentieth-century church than this. It describes vividly the respectable, sentimental, nominal, skin-deep religiosity which is so widespread among us today. Our Christianity is flabby and anemic. We appear to have taken a lukewarm bath of religion." How would you describe your church's spiritual temperature—hot, cold, or lukewarm? Why? How would you describe your own faith temperature?

_____

_____

_____

12) The church at Sardis had a reputation for being spiritually alive and vibrant, but in reality it was dead. Can you think of any ways in which your spiritual _reputation_ exceeds your true spiritual _situation_? How is God calling you to change?

_____

_____

_____

13) The church at Philadelphia was commended for keeping Christ's word and for persevering in the face of trouble and hardship. What qualities do you think Christ might affirm in _your_ life?

_____

_____

_____

## Personal Response

Write out additional reflections, questions you may have, or a prayer.

_____

_____

_____

_____

# 4

# A Vision of Christ in Heaven
### *Revelation 4:1–5:14*

## Drawing Near

Name several common misconceptions people have about heaven.

_____

_____

_____

Imagine actually seeing Jesus and actually being in His presence for eternity. What thoughts and feelings come to your mind?

_____

_____

_____

What does it mean to you to worship God?

_____

_____

_____

## The Context

Christians and non-Christians alike seem to be fascinated these days with the afterlife. Television programs explore the mysterious realm of the supernatural, often focusing on angels or demons and their alleged interaction with humans. Many people claim to have had near-death experiences.

In contrast to the fanciful, bizarre, and often silly fabrications of those who falsely claim to have visited heaven, the Bible records the accounts of two people who actually were taken there in visions. In 2 Corinthians 12 the apostle Paul wrote of being transported to the third heaven (the abode of God). But he was forbidden to speak of what he saw there (2 Cor. 12:4). The apostle John also had the inestimable privilege of visiting heaven. John was permitted to give a detailed description of his vision, which he did in chapters 4 and 5 of Revelation. In these two chapters, John recorded the second vision he saw.

The Bible refers to heaven more than five hundred times. Yet John's description in these chapters is the most complete and informative in all of Scripture. Through John's vision, believers have the privilege of previewing the place where they will live forever.

## KEYS TO THE TEXT

*Twenty-four Elders:* The elders' joint rule with Christ, their white garments, and their golden crowns all seem to indicate that these twenty-four people represent the redeemed (see vv. 9–11; 5:5–14; 7:11–17; 11:16–18; 14:3; 19:4). But which redeemed? Here the elders are best understood as being representatives of the church, which sings the song of redemption (5:8–10). They are the overcomers who have their crowns and live in the place prepared for them, where they have gone to be with Jesus.

*Four Living Creatures:* The term in Revelation is literally "four living ones or beings." These are the cherubim, those angels frequently referred to in the Old Testament in connection with God's presence, power, and holiness. Although John's description is not identical to the prophet Ezekiel's, they are obviously both referring to the same supernatural and indescribable beings (Ps. 80:1; 99:1; see Ezek. 1:4–25; 10:15).

## UNLEASHING THE TEXT

Read 4:1–5:14, noting the key words and definitions next to the passage.

### Revelation 4:1–5:14 (NKJV)

**Come up here** (v. 1)—This is not a veiled reference to the rapture of the church, but a command for John to be temporarily transported to heaven "in the Spirit" to receive revelation about future events.

**things which must take place after this** (v. 1)—According to the outline given in 1:19, this

**4:1** *After these things I looked, and behold, a door standing open in heaven. And the first voice which I heard was like a trumpet speaking with me, saying, "Come up here, and I will show you things which must take place after this."*

**2** *Immediately I was in the Spirit; and behold, a throne set in heaven, and One sat on the throne.*

begins the third and final section of the book, describing the events that will follow the Church age.

**throne** (v. 2)—This refers not so much to a piece of furniture as it does to a symbol of sovereign rule and authority (7:15; 11:19; 16:17–18). It is the focus of chapter four, occurring thirteen times, with eleven times referring to God's throne.

3 *And He who sat there was like a jasper and a sardius stone in appearance; and there was a rainbow around the throne, in appearance like an emerald.*

4 *Around the throne were twenty-four thrones, and on the thrones I saw twenty-four elders sitting, clothed in white robes; and they had crowns of gold on their heads.*

5 *And from the throne proceeded lightnings, thunderings, and voices. Seven lamps of fire were burning before the throne, which are the seven Spirits of God.*

6 *Before the throne there was a sea of glass, like crystal. And in the midst of the throne, and around the throne, were four living creatures full of eyes in front and in back.*

7 *The first living creature was like a lion, the second living creature like a calf, the third living creature had a face like a man, and the fourth living creature was like a flying eagle.*

8 *The four living creatures, each having six wings, were full of eyes around and within. And they do not rest day or night, saying: "Holy, holy, holy, Lord God Almighty, Who was and is and is to come!"*

9 *Whenever the living creatures give glory and honor and thanks to Him who sits on the throne, who lives forever and ever,*

**jasper** (v. 3)—John later describes this stone as "crystal clear" (21:11), probably referring to a diamond, which refracts all the colors of the spectrum in wondrous brilliance.

**sardius** (v. 3)—a fiery bright ruby stone named for the city near which it was found

**emerald** (v. 3)—A cool, emerald-green hue dominates the multicolored rainbow surrounding God's throne. From the time of Noah, the rainbow became a sign of God's faithfulness to His Word, His promises, and His Noahic covenant (Gen. 9:12–17).

**lightnings, thunderings** (v. 5)—not the fury of nature, but the firestorm of righteous fury about to come from an awesome, powerful God upon a sinful world (8:5; 11:19; 16:18)

**seven Spirits of God** (v. 5)—the Holy Spirit

**sea of glass** (v. 6)—There is no sea in heaven (21:1), but the crystal pavement that serves as the floor of God's throne stretches out like a great, glistening sea.

**full of eyes** (v. 6)—Although not omniscient—an attribute reserved for God alone—these four living creatures, angels, have a comprehensive knowledge and perception. Nothing escapes their scrutiny (see v. 8).

**first . . . like a lion** (v. 7)—In what is obviously intended as symbolic language, John compares these four beings to four of God's earthly creations. Ezekiel indicates that every cherub has these four attributes. The likeness to a lion symbolizes strength and power.

**second . . . like a calf** (v. 7)—The image of a calf demonstrates that these beings render humble service to God.

**third . . . face like a man** (v. 7)—Their likeness to man shows they are rational beings.

**fourth . . . like a flying eagle** (v. 7)—The cherubim fulfill their service to God with the swiftness of eagles' wings.

**Holy, holy, holy** (v. 8)—Often God is extoled for His holiness in this threefold form, because it is the summation of all that He is—His most prominent attribute.

**cast their crowns** (v. 10)—Aware that God alone is responsible for the rewards they have received, they divest themselves of all honor and cast it at the feet of their King (see 2:10).

**You created all things** (v. 11)—It is the Creator God who set out to redeem His creation.

**written inside and on the back** (v. 1)—This is typical of various kinds of contracts in the ancient world, including deeds, marriage contracts, rental and lease agreements, and wills. The inside of the scroll contained all the details of the contract, and the outside—or back—contained a summary of the document. In this case, it is almost certainly a deed—the title deed to the earth (see Jer. 32:7–15).

**sealed with seven seals** (v. 1)—Romans sealed their wills seven times—on the edge at each roll—to prevent unauthorized entry. Hebrew title deeds required a minimum of three witnesses and three separate seals, with more important transactions requiring more witnesses and seals.

**strong angel** (v. 2)—The identity of this angel is uncertain, but it may refer to the angel Gabriel, whose name means "strength of God."

10 the twenty-four elders fall down before Him who sits on the throne and worship Him who lives forever and ever, and cast their crowns before the throne, saying:

11 "You are worthy, O Lord, to receive glory and honor and power; for You created all things, and by Your will they exist and were created."

5:1 And I saw in the right hand of Him who sat on the throne a scroll written inside and on the back, sealed with seven seals.

2 Then I saw a strong angel proclaiming with a loud voice, "Who is worthy to open the scroll and to loose its seals?"

3 And no one in heaven or on the earth or under the earth was able to open the scroll, or to look at it.

4 So I wept much, because no one was found worthy to open and read the scroll, or to look at it.

5 But one of the elders said to me, "Do not weep. Behold, the Lion of the tribe of Judah, the Root of David, has prevailed to open the scroll and to loose its seven seals."

6 And I looked, and behold, in the midst of the throne and of the four living creatures, and in the midst of the elders, stood a Lamb as though it had been

**heaven or on the earth or under the earth** (v. 3)—A common biblical expression denoting the entire universe and not intended to teach three precise divisions.

**the Lion of the tribe of Judah** (v. 5)—One of the earliest titles for the Messiah (see Gen. 49:8–10), it speaks of His fierceness and strength, which although glimpsed in His first coming, do not appear in their fullness until the moment anticipated here.

**the Root of David** (v. 5)—Another clearly messianic title (see Isa. 11:1–10), it anticipates His being a descendant of David, who with devastating force will compel the wicked of the earth to succumb to His authority.

**Lamb** (v. 6)—Hearing of a lion, John turns to see a lamb (literally "a little lamb"). God required the Jews to bring the Passover lamb into their houses for four days, essentially making it a pet, before it was to be violently slain. This is the true Passover Lamb, God's Son.

**as though it had been slain** (v. 6)—The scars from its slaughter are still clearly visible, but it is standing—it is alive.

**seven horns** (v. 6)—In Scripture, horns always symbolize power, because in the animal kingdom they are used to exert power and inflict wounds in combat. Seven horns signify complete or perfect power. Unlike other defenseless lambs, this One has complete, sovereign power.

slain, having seven horns and seven eyes, which are the seven Spirits of God sent out into all the earth.

7 Then He came and took the scroll out of the right hand of Him who sat on the throne.

8 Now when He had taken the scroll, the four living creatures and the twenty-four elders fell down before the Lamb, each having a harp, and golden bowls full of incense, which are the prayers of the saints.

9 And they sang a new song, saying: "You are worthy to take the scroll, and to open its seals; for You were slain, and have redeemed us to God by Your blood out of every tribe and tongue and people and nation,

10 And have made us kings and priests to our God; and we shall reign on the earth."

11 Then I looked, and I heard the voice of many angels around the throne, the living creatures, and the elders; and the number of them was ten thousand times ten thousand, and thousands of thousands,

12 saying with a loud voice: "Worthy is the Lamb who was slain to receive power and riches and wisdom, and strength and honor and glory and blessing!"

13 And every creature which is in heaven and on the earth and under the earth and such as are in the sea, and all that are in them, I heard saying: "Blessing and honor and glory and power be to Him who sits on the throne, and to the Lamb, forever and ever!"

14 Then the four living creatures said, "Amen!" And the twenty-four elders fell down and worshiped Him who lives forever and ever.

**harp** (v. 8)—These ancient stringed instruments not only accompanied the songs of God's people (1 Chron. 25:6; Ps. 33:2), but also accompanied prophecy (see 1 Sam. 10:5). The twenty-four elders, representative of the redeemed Church, played their harps in praise and in a symbolic indication that all the prophets had said was about to be fulfilled.

**bowls full of incense** (v. 8)—These golden, wide-mouth saucers were common in the tabernacle and temple. Incense was a normal part of the Old Testament ritual. Priests stood twice daily before the inner veil of the temple and burned incense so that the smoke would carry into the Holy of Holies and be swept into the nostrils of God. This symbolized the people's prayers rising to Him.

**prayers of the saints** (v. 8)—Specifically, these prayers represent all that the redeemed have ever prayed concerning ultimate and final redemption. This becomes a major theme throughout the book (see 11:17–18; 13:7, 9–10; 14:12; 16:6; 17:6; 18:20, 24; 19:8; 20:9).

**new song** (v. 9)—The Old Testament is filled with references to a new song that flows from a heart that has experienced God's redemption and deliverance (see 14:3; Ps. 33:3; 96:1; 144:9). This new song anticipates the final, glorious redemption that God is about to begin.

**redeemed us to God by Your blood** (v. 9)—The sacrificial death of Christ on behalf of sinners made Him worthy to take the scroll.

**ten thousand times ten thousand** (v. 11)—Literally "myriads of myriads," this number is intended to express an amount beyond calculation. The Greek expression can also be translated "innumerable" (Luke 12:1; Heb. 12:22).

**power . . . and blessing** (v. 12)—This doxology records seven qualities intrinsic to God and to the Lamb that demand our praise.

1) How did John describe the One "sitting on the throne"?

_____

_____

_____

_____

*(Verses to consider: Dan. 7:9–10)*

2) What creatures did John see around the throne? What were they doing?

_____

_____

_____

3) What is the identity and significance of the Lamb in Revelation 5 that John saw standing?

_____

_____

_____

*(Verses to consider: Exod. 12:1–6; Isa. 53:7; John 1:29; 1 Pet. 1:18–19)*

4) Why was Christ worthy to take the scroll in chapter 5?

_____

_____

_____

5) Describe the worship directed toward the Lamb in chapter 5. What is the mood around the throne?

_____

_____

_____

## Going Deeper

The Old Testament prophet Ezekiel experienced amazing visions of living creatures similar to John's vision. Read Ezekiel 1:4–14, 26–28.

4 *Then I looked, and behold, a whirlwind was coming out of the north, a great cloud with raging fire engulfing itself; and brightness was all around it and radiating out of its midst like the color of amber, out of the midst of the fire.*

5 *Also from within it came the likeness of four living creatures. And this was their appearance: they had the likeness of a man.*

6 *Each one had four faces, and each one had four wings.*

7 *Their legs were straight, and the soles of their feet were like the soles of calves' feet. They sparkled like the color of burnished bronze.*

8 *The hands of a man were under their wings on their four sides; and each of the four had faces and wings.*

9 *Their wings touched one another. The creatures did not turn when they went, but each one went straight forward.*

10 *As for the likeness of their faces, each had the face of a man; each of the four had the face of a lion on the right side, each of the four had the face of an ox on the left side, and each of the four had the face of an eagle.*

11 *Thus were their faces. Their wings stretched upward; two wings of each one touched one another, and two covered their bodies.*

12 *And each one went straight forward; they went wherever the spirit wanted to go, and they did not turn when they went.*

13 *As for the likeness of the living creatures, their appearance was like burning coals of fire, like the appearance of torches going back and forth among the living creatures. The fire was bright, and out of the fire went lightning.*

14 *And the living creatures ran back and forth, in appearance like a flash of lightning. . . .*

26 *And above the firmament over their heads was the likeness of a throne, in appearance like a sapphire stone; on the likeness of the throne was a likeness with the appearance of a man high above it.*

27 *Also from the appearance of His waist and upward I saw, as it were, the color of amber with the appearance of fire all around within it; and from the appearance of His waist and downward I saw, as it were, the appearance of fire with brightness all around.*

28 *Like the appearance of a rainbow in a cloud on a rainy day, so was the appearance of the brightness all around it. This was the appearance of the likeness of the glory of the* Lord.

## Exploring the Meaning

6) Compare the picture of the living creatures and the man on the throne in Ezekiel 1 with John's vision in Revelation 4–5. What similarities do you find?

_____

_____

_____

_____

7) What feeling do you get when you read these descriptions of symbolic heavenly scenes? What is the tone?

_____

_____

_____

_____

8) What do you learn about worship from these passages?

_____

_____

_____

_____

9) Read Matthew 17:6. What is the common posture of those who witness the glory of God? Why?

_____

_____

_____

_____

*(Verses to consider: Gen. 17:3; Josh. 5:14; Ezek. 44:4; Acts 9:4)*

10) Read Psalm 96:1–4. Many scenes in Revelation are filled with praise and singing. What part does singing praises play in worshiping God? Why is it such an integral part?

_____

_____

_____

_____

*(Verses to consider: Judg. 5:3; 2 Chron. 5:13; Neh. 12:46;*
*Ps. 7:17; 9:1–2; 40:3; 146:2; Isa. 42:10; Acts 16:25; Eph. 5:19; Rev. 14:3)*

## TRUTH FOR TODAY

The events described in these two chapters anticipate the holocaust of divine judgment about to be poured out on the sinful, rebellious, cursed earth (Rev. 6–19). Awestruck by the indescribable majesty of God's throne, and the flashes of lightning and peals of thunder that proceed from it, the cherubim and elders begin a series of hymns of praise to God. Those hymns celebrate God as Creator and Redeemer, rejoicing that He is about to take back what is rightfully His. This is the moment that all Christians and the entire creation long for.

## REFLECTING ON THE TEXT

11) How can glimpsing true worship in heaven help us better worship here on earth?

_____

_____

_____

_____

12) Describe your own habits of worship. Is it passionate and exuberant? Or is it restrained and distracted? Why?

_____

_____

_____

_____

13) Knowing that the redeemed in heaven will include people from "every tribe and tongue and people and nation" (5:9), what should our attitude be toward other races, countries, and cultures?

_____

_____

_____

_____

14) What new insights have you gained into heaven from this study? How can this affect your life today so that you have more of an eternal perspective?

_____

_____

_____

_____

## PERSONAL RESPONSE

Write out additional reflections, questions you may have, or a prayer.

_____

_____

_____

_____

_____

_____

_____

_____

_____

_____

# 5

# OPENING THE SEALS
*Revelation 6:1–7:17*

## DRAWING NEAR

We've all seen cartoons of a wild-eyed, bearded prophet holding up a sign that says: "Repent! The end is near!" Why is that type of thing often laughed at?

_____

_____

_____

_____

Do you believe in a final judgment? Why or why not?

_____

_____

_____

_____

## THE CONTEXT

The Bible teaches that the world is headed inexorably toward a final, cataclysmic war called the Battle of Armageddon. Until that climactic holocaust, things will continue to deteriorate as the world falls deeper and deeper into chaos, confusion, and sin. As the end approaches, wars will increase, crime will escalate, there will be economic upheavals, and the world will experience unprecedented natural disasters, such as earthquakes, floods, famines, and diseases. All those calamities will mark the outpouring of God's wrath on the fallen, rebellious world.

In Revelation 5:1–7, the setting is heaven, where Christ received from God the Father a scroll sealed with seven seals until opened by the One with authority to do so. Beginning in chapter 6, the scene shifts to earth and the effects of the scroll being unrolled and its seals broken. The unrolling of the scroll marks the beginning of God's wrath and judgment on sinful mankind as the Lord takes back creation from the usurper, Satan.

## KEYS TO THE TEXT

*The Seals:* In chapter 5, Christ was the only One found worthy to open the little scroll—the title deed to the universe. As he breaks the seven seals that secure the scroll, each seal unleashes a new demonstration of God's judgment on the earth in the future tribulation period. These seal judgments include all the judgments to the end. The seventh seal contains the seven trumpets; the seventh trumpet contains the seven bowls.

Each of the scroll's seven seals represents a specific divine judgment that will be poured out sequentially on the earth. The seals encompass the entire seven-year period of the Tribulation, culminating with the return of Christ. It seems best to understand the first four seals as taking place during the first half of the Tribulation. The events of the fifth seal will mark the midpoint, and then the events of the sixth and seventh seals will stretch into the second half of the seven-year period of the Tribulation.

*Great Tribulation:* A seven-year period of intense judgment on the earth. The exact phrase, "the great tribulation," is found only once in the Bible, here in 7:14. The Great Tribulation is to be distinguished from the general tribulation a believer faces in the world (Matt. 13:21; John 16:33; Acts 14:22). It is also to be distinguished from God's specific wrath upon the unbelieving world at the end of the age (Mark 13:24; Rom. 2:5–10; 2 Thess. 1:6). The Great Tribulation fulfills Daniel's prophecies (Dan. 7–12). It will be a time of evil from false christs and false prophets, and natural disasters will occur throughout the world (Matt. 24:21; Mark 13:22). The second half of the Tribulation will feature the Day of the Lord, in which God unleashes His judgment and wrath on the earth in intensifying waves. Though it is a time of unparalleled judgment, it is also a time of unparalleled grace in salvation (see Matt. 24:12–14).

## UNLEASHING THE TEXT

Read 6:1–7:17, noting the key words and definitions next to the passage.

*white horse* (v. 2)—The animal represents an unparalleled time of world peace—a false peace that is to be short-lived (see v. 4). This peace will be ushered in by a series of false messiahs, culminating with the Antichrist.

### Revelation 6:1–7:17 (NKJV)

6:1 *Now I saw when the Lamb opened one of the seals; and I heard one of the four living creatures saying with a voice like thunder, "Come and see."*

2 *And I looked, and behold, a white horse. He who sat*

on it had a bow; and a crown was given to him, and he went out conquering and to conquer.

3 When He opened the second seal, I heard the second living creature saying, "Come and see."

4 Another horse, fiery red, went out. And it was granted to the one who sat on it to take peace from the earth, and that people should kill one another; and there was given to him a great sword.

5 When He opened the third seal, I heard the third living creature say, "Come and see." So I looked, and behold, a black horse, and he who sat on it had a pair of scales in his hand.

6 And I heard a voice in the midst of the four living creatures saying, "A quart of wheat for a denarius, and three quarts of barley for a denarius; and do not harm the oil and the wine."

7 When He opened the fourth seal, I heard the voice of the fourth living creature saying, "Come and see."

8 So I looked, and behold, a pale horse. And the name

**He who sat on it** (v. 2)—The four horses and their riders do not represent specific individuals, but forces. Some, however, identify this rider with Antichrist. Although he will be the leading figure, John's point is that the entire world will follow him, being obsessed with pursuing this false peace.

**bow** (v. 2)—The bow is a symbol of war, but the absence of arrows implies that this victory is a bloodless one—a peace won by covenant and agreement, not by war.

**crown** (v. 2)—This word refers to the kind of laurel wreath awarded winning athletes. It "was given to him." Antichrist becomes king, elected by the world's inhabitants regardless of the cost, and will conquer the entire earth in a bloodless coup.

**Another horse, fiery red** (v. 4)—Its blood-red appearance speaks of the holocaust of war (see Matt. 24:7). God will grant this horse and its rider the power to create worldwide war. But as horrible as this judgment is, it will be only the "birth pains," the beginning pains of God's wrath.

**people should kill one another** (v. 4)—Violent slaughter will become commonplace.

**sword** (v. 4)—Not the long, broad sword, but the shorter, more easily maneuvered one that assassins often used and that soldiers carried into battle. It depicts assassination, revolt, massacre, and wholesale slaughter.

**black horse** (v. 5)—Black signifies famine (see Lam. 5:8–10). Worldwide war will destroy the food supply and spawn global hunger.

**pair of scales** (v. 5)—The common measuring device—two small trays hung from each end of a balance beam—indicates that the scarcity of food will lead to rationing and food lines.

**quart of wheat** (v. 6)—the approximate amount necessary to sustain one person for one day

**denarius** (v. 6)—one day's normal wages; one day's work will provide enough food for only one person

**three quarts of barley** (v. 6)—Usually fed to animals, this grain was low in nutrients and cheaper than wheat. A day's wages provides enough for only a small family's daily supply.

**oil and the wine** (v. 6)—Although the point could be that these foods will not be affected by the famine, a more straightforward meaning is that bare staples—oil was used in the preparation of bread, and wine was considered necessary for cooking and purifying water—suddenly will become luxuries that have to be carefully protected.

**pale horse** (v. 8)—*Chloros*, the Greek word from which the English word "chlorophyll" comes, describes the pale, ashen-green pallor characteristic of the decomposition of a corpse. God grants this horseman the authority to bring death to twenty-five percent of the world's population. Hades (v. 8)—the place of the dead, which is identified as a common and fitting partner for death (20:13; see 1:18)

**fifth seal** (v. 9)—This seal describes the force of the saints' prayers for God's vengeance. Its events will begin in the first half and mark the mid-point and events following, in the seven-year period that is called the Great Tribulation (2:22; 7:14; see Matt. 24:9, 15; Dan. 9:24–27; 2 Thess. 2:4). The second three-and-one-half-year period (11:2; 12:6; 13:5) features the Day of the Lord, in which God unleashes His judgment and wrath on the earth in intensifying waves (see 1 Thess. 5:2).

**under the altar** (v. 9)—probably a reference to the altar of incense, which pictured the saints' prayers ascending to God (5:8)

**the souls of those who had been slain** (v. 9)—Christians martyred for their faith (see 7:9, 13–15; 17:6)

**rest a little while longer** (v. 11)—God will answer their prayer for vengeance, but in His time.

of him who sat on it was Death, and Hades followed with him. And power was given to them over a fourth of the earth, to kill with sword, with hunger, with death, and by the beasts of the earth.

9 When He opened the fifth seal, I saw under the altar the souls of those who had been slain for the word of God and for the testimony which they held.

10 And they cried with a loud voice, saying, "How long, O Lord, holy and true, until You judge and avenge our blood on those who dwell on the earth?"

11 Then a white robe was given to each of them; and it was said to them that they should rest a little while longer, until both the number of their fellow servants and their brethren, who would be killed as they were, was completed.

12 I looked when He opened the sixth seal, and behold, there was a great earthquake; and the sun became black as sackcloth of hair, and the moon became like blood.

13 And the stars of heaven fell to the earth, as a fig tree drops its late figs when it is shaken by a mighty wind.

**until . . . the number . . . was completed** (v. 11)—God has predetermined the number of the righteous, whose death He will allow before moving to destroy the rebels.

**sixth seal** (v. 12)—The force described in this seal is overpowering fear (see Luke 21:26). While the first five seals will result from human activity that God uses to accomplish His purposes, with the opening of the sixth seal He begins direct intervention. The previous five seals will be precursors to the full fury of the Day of the Lord, which will begin with the sixth seal (v. 17). The events described in this seal unleash the seventh, which contains the trumpet judgments (ch. 8, 9; 11:15–18:24) and the bowl judgments (ch. 16).

**great earthquake** (v. 12)—There have been many earthquakes prior to this (Matt. 24:7), but this will be more than an earthquake. All the earth's faults will begin to fracture simultaneously, resulting in a cataclysmic, global earthquake.

**moon became like blood** (v. 12)—Accompanying the earthquake will be numerous volcanic eruptions; and large amounts of ash and debris will be blown into the earth's atmosphere, blackening the sun and giving the moon a blood-red hue.

**stars of heaven fell** (v. 13)—In Greek the word "stars" can refer to any celestial body, large or small, and is not limited to normal English usage. The best explanation is a massive asteroid or meteor shower.

**late figs** (v. 13)—winter figs that grow without the protection of leaves and are easily blown from the tree

14 *Then the sky receded as a scroll when it is rolled up,
and every mountain and island was moved out of
its place.*

15 *And the kings of the earth, the great men, the rich
men, the commanders, the mighty men, every slave
and every free man, hid themselves in the caves and
in the rocks of the mountains,*

16 *and said to the mountains and rocks, "Fall on us
and hide us from the face of Him who sits on the
throne and from the wrath of the Lamb!*

17 *For the great day of His wrath has come, and who is
able to stand?"*

7:1 *After these things I saw four angels standing at the
four corners of the earth, holding the four winds
of the earth, that the wind should not blow on the
earth, on the sea, or on any tree.*

2 *Then I saw another angel ascending from the east,
having the seal of the living God. And he cried
with a loud voice to the four angels to whom it was
granted to harm the earth and the sea,*

3 *saying, "Do not harm the earth, the sea, or the trees
till we have sealed the servants of our God on their
foreheads."*

4 *And I heard the number of those who were sealed.
One hundred and forty-four thousand of all the
tribes of the children of Israel were sealed:*

5 *of the tribe of Judah twelve thousand were sealed; of
the tribe of Reuben twelve thousand were sealed; of
the tribe of Gad twelve thousand were sealed;*

6 *of the tribe of Asher twelve thousand were sealed; of
the tribe of Naphtali twelve thousand were sealed;
of the tribe of Manasseh twelve thousand were
sealed;*

***sky receded as a scroll*** (v. 14)—
The earth's atmosphere will be
somehow dramatically affected
and the sky as we know it dis-
appears.

***every mountain and island
was moved*** (v. 14)—Under
the stress created by the global
earthquake, great segments of
the earth's plates will begin to
slip and shift, realigning whole
continents.

***wrath of the Lamb*** (v. 16)—
Earth's inhabitants will recognize for the first time the source
of all their trouble. Incredibly,
prior to this they will be living
life as usual.

***great day*** (v. 17)—The sixth seal
will commence what the prophets call "the Day of the Lord."

***four corners*** (7:1)—the four
quadrants of the compass; that
is, the angels will take up key
positions on earth

***four winds*** (v. 1)—This is a figurative expression, indicating all
the earth's winds—those from
south, east, north, and west. The
four angels will turn off, for a
brief interlude, the essential en-
gine of our earth's atmosphere.

***seal of the living God*** (v. 2)—A
"seal" often refers to a signet
ring used to press its image into
wax melted on a document.
The resulting imprint implied
authenticity and ownership
and protected the contents (see
9:4). In this case, the mark is the
name of God (14:1).

***One hundred and forty-four
thousand*** (v. 4)—This refers to
a missionary corps of redeemed
Jews who are instrumental in

the salvation of many Jews and Gentiles during the Tribulation (vv. 9–17). They will be the firstfruits
of a new redeemed Israel (v. 4; Zech. 12:10). Israel will finally be the witness nation she refused to be
in the Old Testament (see Rom. 11:25–27).

***all the tribes of the children of Israel*** (v. 4)—By sovereign election, God will seal twelve thousand from
each of the twelve tribes, promising His protection while they accomplish their mission.

7 *of the tribe of Simeon twelve thousand were sealed; of the tribe of Levi twelve thousand were sealed; of the tribe of Issachar twelve thousand were sealed;*

8 *of the tribe of Zebulun twelve thousand were sealed; of the tribe of Joseph twelve thousand were sealed; of the tribe of Benjamin twelve thousand were sealed.*

9 *After these things I looked, and behold, a great multitude which no one could number, of all nations, tribes, peoples, and tongues, standing before the throne and before the Lamb, clothed with white robes, with palm branches in their hands,*

10 *and crying out with a loud voice, saying, "Salvation belongs to our God who sits on the throne, and to the Lamb!"*

11 *All the angels stood around the throne and the elders and the four living creatures, and fell on their faces before the throne and worshiped God,*

12 *saying: "Amen! Blessing and glory and wisdom, Thanksgiving and honor and power and might, be to our God forever and ever. Amen."*

13 *Then one of the elders answered, saying to me, "Who are these arrayed in white robes, and where did they come from?"*

14 *And I said to him, "Sir, you know." So he said to me, "These are the ones who come out of the great tribulation, and washed their robes and made them white in the blood of the Lamb.*

15 *Therefore they are before the throne of God, and serve Him day and night in His temple. And He who sits on the throne will dwell among them.*

**a great multitude** (v. 9)—While the tribulation period will be a time of judgment, it will also be a time of unprecedented redemption (see v. 14; 6:9–11; 20:4; Isa. 11:10; Matt. 24:14).

**all nations, tribes, peoples, and tongues** (v. 9)—all the earth's people groups

**palm branches** (v. 9)—in ancient times, they were associated with celebrations, including the Feast of Tabernacles (Lev. 23:40; Neh. 8:17; John 12:13)

**Salvation belongs to our God** (v. 10)—Salvation is the theme of their worship, and they recognize that it comes solely from Him.

**the great tribulation** (v. 14)—See 3:10; 6:1, 9, 12. These people didn't go with the raptured church, since they were not yet saved. During the seven-year period they will be saved, martyred, and enter heaven. Though it is a time of unparalleled judgment, it is also a time of unparalleled grace in salvation (see Matt. 24:12–14).

**washed their robes** (v. 14)—See 19:8. Salvation's cleansing is in view.

**blood of the Lamb** (v. 14)—This refers to the atoning sacrifice of Christ (see 1:5; 5:9).

**His temple** (v. 15)—This refers to the heavenly throne of God (see 11:19). During the millennium there will also be a temple on earth—a special holy place where God dwells in a partially restored, but still fallen, universe (see Ezek. 40–48). In the final, eternal state with its new heavens and earth, there is no temple; God Himself, who will fill all, will be its temple (21:22).

**dwell among them** (v. 15)—The preferred reading is that He "will spread His tent over them." God's presence will become their canopy of shelter to protect them from all the terrors of a fallen world and the indescribable horrors they have experienced on the earth during the time of tribulation.

<sup>16</sup> *They shall neither hunger anymore nor thirst anymore; the sun shall not strike them, nor any heat;*

<sup>17</sup> *for the Lamb who is in the midst of the throne will shepherd them and lead them to living fountains of waters. And God will wipe away every tear from their eyes."*

**shepherd** (v. 17)—In a beautiful mix of images, the Lamb has always been the Shepherd.

1) The first seal depicts a time of worldwide peace. How will this aid in lulling the people of earth into a false sense of security?

_____

_____

_____

_____

*(Verses to consider: Dan. 9:24–27; 1 Thess. 5:3)*

2) What kind of judgment did the breaking of the second and third seals unleash upon the earth?

_____

_____

_____

_____

_____

*(Verses to consider: Dan. 11:36–45; Mark 13:7, 8; Luke 21:9)*

3) What will be the results of the breaking of the third, fourth, and fifth seals?

_____

_____

_____

_____

_____

4) What did John see when the sixth seal was broken?

_____

_____

_____

5) Who will be in heaven worshiping together? Describe the tone of this scene (7:9–12).

_____

_____

_____

_____

6) What is promised to those who endure (7:13–17)?

_____

_____

_____

_____

## GOING DEEPER

When Jesus' disciples asked Him what would be the signs of the end of the age, Jesus mentioned many things similar to John's vision in Revelation. Read Matthew 24:6–33.

6   "And you will hear of wars and rumors of wars. See that you are not troubled; for all these things must come to pass, but the end is not yet.

7   For nation will rise against nation, and kingdom against kingdom. And there will be famines, pestilences, and earthquakes in various places.

8   All these are the beginning of sorrows.

9   "Then they will deliver you up to tribulation and kill you, and you will be hated by all nations for My name's sake.

10  And then many will be offended, will betray one another, and will hate one another.

11  Then many false prophets will rise up and deceive many.

12  And because lawlessness will abound, the love of many will grow cold.

13  But he who endures to the end shall be saved.

14 *And this gospel of the kingdom will be preached in all the world as a witness to all the nations, and then the end will come.*

15 *"Therefore when you see the 'abomination of desolation,' spoken of by Daniel the prophet, standing in the holy place" (whoever reads, let him understand),*

16 *"then let those who are in Judea flee to the mountains.*

17 *Let him who is on the housetop not go down to take anything out of his house.*

18 *And let him who is in the field not go back to get his clothes.*

19 *But woe to those who are pregnant and to those who are nursing babies in those days!*

20 *And pray that your flight may not be in winter or on the Sabbath.*

21 *For then there will be great tribulation, such as has not been since the beginning of the world until this time, no, nor ever shall be.*

22 *And unless those days were shortened, no flesh would be saved; but for the elect's sake those days will be shortened.*

23 *"Then if anyone says to you, 'Look, here is the Christ!' or 'There!' do not believe it.*

24 *For false christs and false prophets will rise and show great signs and wonders to deceive, if possible, even the elect.*

25 *See, I have told you beforehand.*

26 *"Therefore if they say to you, 'Look, He is in the desert!' do not go out; or 'Look, He is in the inner rooms!' do not believe it.*

27 *For as the lightning comes from the east and flashes to the west, so also will the coming of the Son of Man be.*

28 *For wherever the carcass is, there the eagles will be gathered together.*

29 *"Immediately after the tribulation of those days the sun will be darkened, and the moon will not give its light; the stars will fall from heaven, and the powers of the heavens will be shaken.*

30 *Then the sign of the Son of Man will appear in heaven, and then all the tribes of the earth will mourn, and they will see the Son of Man coming on the clouds of heaven with power and great glory.*

31 *And He will send His angels with a great sound of a trumpet, and they will gather together His elect from the four winds, from one end of heaven to the other.*

32 *"Now learn this parable from the fig tree: When its branch has already become tender and puts forth leaves, you know that summer is near.*

33 *So you also, when you see all these things, know that it is near—at the doors!*

## Exploring the Meaning

7) What destructive events in nature will come at the end of the age?

_____

_____

_____

_____

8) How do these future events described by Christ dovetail with the events depicted in Revelation 6 and 7?

_____

_____

_____

_____

9) Read 2 Thessalonians 1:6–10. Compare what it reveals to John's description of events surrounding the breaking of the fifth seal (Rev. 6:9–11).

_____

_____

_____

_____

10) Read Joel 2:28–32. How does this Old Testament prophecy of the great and terrible Day of the Lord compare to the description by John in Revelation 6:12–17?

_____

_____

_____

_____

## TRUTH FOR TODAY

While Scripture reveals that God is loving, merciful, and gracious—the Savior of sinners—one truth about Him that is decidedly unpopular today is that He is a God of vengeance against those who reject both Him and salvation in His Son. The Bible repeatedly affirms that to be the case. God's vengeance is not to be equated with petty human vindictiveness and bitter desire for revenge. God's holiness, righteousness, and justice demand that He take vengeance on unrepentant sinners. Vengeance belongs to God alone because all sin is ultimately against Him and an offense to Him.

## REFLECTING ON THE TEXT

11) The unleashing of divine judgment after the breaking of the fifth seal brings to mind the subject of the age-old persecution of God's people. In what ways have you experienced animosity from unbelievers because of your faith? How can you better glorify God in the future in the midst of such circumstances?

_____

_____

_____

_____

12) As you study John's vision of the future and ponder all that is to come, how specifically are you motivated, challenged, and convicted to:

Walk with Christ more closely?

Share your faith with others?

Worship God?

Study the Word?

_____

_____

_____

_____

_____

## Personal Response

Write out additional reflections, questions you may have, or a prayer.

# 6

# GOD'S TRUMPETS
*Revelation 8:1–9:21*

## DRAWING NEAR

A new Christian confides in you: "I'm reading the book of Revelation and, frankly, I don't understand most of it. But I *do* understand that the notes in my study Bible clearly say that all these *terrible* judgments will be poured out on unbelievers—maybe even some of my friends! Do you believe that? I'm having a hard time believing that a loving God could do that to His beloved creatures!" How do you respond?

_____

_____

_____

_____

_____

## THE CONTEXT

The first five seals (false peace, war, famine, death, and vengeance) describe the preliminary judgments leading to the full outpouring of divine wrath. As horrifying as those preliminary judgments are, they pale before the terrors of the sixth seal, which marks the beginning of the Day of the Lord. So terrifying are the judgments of the sixth seal that people are finally forced to acknowledge God as the Source of the calamities. At that point they will cry "to the mountains and rocks, 'Fall on us and hide us from the face of Him who sits on the throne and from the wrath of the Lamb! For the great day of His wrath has come, and who is able to stand?'" (6:16–17).

When the Lamb opens the seventh and last seal on the scroll, the judgments of the Day of the Lord will intensify and expand dramatically. This final seal contains the trumpet and bowl judgments. While the exact timetable for these judgments is not revealed, their escalating devastation indicates they all occur during the last half of the Great Tribulation. Therefore, the seventh seal encompasses all God's final wrath up to the triumphant return of the Lord Jesus Christ in glory.

## Keys to the Text

*Seven Trumpets:* In Revelation, trumpets primarily announce impending judgment. The trumpets are of greater intensity than the seals but not as destructive as the final bowl judgments will be (see 16:1–21). They occur during the final three and one-half years, but the time of each is indefinite, except the effects of the fifth trumpet judgment, which will last five months (9:10). The first four trumpets announce the divine destruction of earth's ecology (vv. 6–12), while the final three involve demonic devastation of earth's inhabitants (9:1–21; 11:15–19).

*Day of the Lord:* This will be a day of wrath, trouble, distress, devastation, desolation, darkness, gloominess, clouds, thick darkness, trumpet, and alarm (Zeph. 1:15–16, 18). There are nineteen indisputable uses of "the Day of the Lord" in the Old Testament and four uses of it in the New Testament (see Acts 2:20; 2 Thess. 2:2; 2 Pet. 3:10). The Old Testament prophets used "Day of the Lord" to describe near (current) historical judgments or far (future) eschatological divine judgments. Six times it is referred to as the "day of doom" and four times as the "day of vengeance." The New Testament calls it a day of "wrath," day of "visitation," and the "great day of God Almighty" (Rev. 16:14). These are terrifying judgments from God for the overwhelming sinfulness of the world. The future "Day of the Lord" which unleashes God's wrath falls into two parts: (1) the end of the seven-year Tribulation period (Rev. 19:11–21) and (2) the end of the Millennium. These two events are actually 1,000 years apart, and Peter refers to the end of the 1,000-year period in connection with the final "Day of the Lord" (2 Pet. 3:10).

## Unleashing the Text

Read 8:1–9:21, noting the key words and definitions next to the passage.

### Revelation 8:1–9:21 (NKJV)

**the seventh seal** (v. 1)—This seal includes not only an earthquake, but the seven trumpet judgments (8:1–9:21; 11:15–19) and the seven bowl judgments (16:1–21), with the bowl judgments flowing out of the seventh trumpet and coming in rapid succession just before Christ's return.

8:1 *When He opened the seventh seal, there was silence in heaven for about half an hour.*

2 *And I saw the seven angels who stand before God, and to them were given seven trumpets.*

**silence in heaven** (v. 1)—the silence of awe and anticipation at the grim reality of the judgments God is about to unleash

3   *Then another angel, having a golden censer, came and stood at the altar. He was given much incense, that he should offer it with the prayers of all the saints upon the golden altar which was before the throne.*

4   *And the smoke of the incense, with the prayers of the saints, ascended before God from the angel's hand.*

5   *Then the angel took the censer, filled it with fire from the altar, and threw it to the earth. And there were noises, thunderings, lightnings, and an earthquake.*

6   *So the seven angels who had the seven trumpets prepared themselves to sound.*

7   *The first angel sounded: And hail and fire followed, mingled with blood, and they were thrown to the earth. And a third of the trees were burned up, and all green grass was burned up.*

8   *Then the second angel sounded: And something like a great mountain burning with fire was thrown into the sea, and a third of the sea became blood.*

9   *And a third of the living creatures in the sea died, and a third of the ships were destroyed.*

10   *Then the third angel sounded: And a great star fell from heaven, burning like a torch, and it fell on a third of the rivers and on the springs of water.*

11   *The name of the star is Wormwood. A third of the waters became wormwood, and many men died from the water, because it was made bitter.*

12   *Then the fourth angel sounded: And a third of the sun was struck, a third of the moon, and a third of*

**censer** (v. 3)—This refers to a golden pan, suspended on a rope or chain, that was used to transport fiery coals from the brazen altar to the altar of incense, in order to ignite the incense, symbolizing the prayers of the people (5:8). This occurred twice daily at the time of the morning and evening sacrifices.

**an earthquake** (v. 5)—surely of equal or greater intensity than one described in the sixth seal (see 6:12)

**hail and fire followed, mingled with blood** (v. 7)—This may describe volcanic eruptions that could certainly result from the earthquake in verse 5. The steam and water thrown into the sky by such eruptions could easily condense into hail and fall to earth along with the fiery lava. Dust and gases may so contaminate falling water that it appears blood red.

**a third of the trees were burned up** (v. 7)—The lava storm will create a blazing fire that devastates one-third of the earth's forests.

**like a great mountain** (v. 8)—Probably a huge meteor or asteroid surrounded by gases that will ignite as it enters earth's atmosphere. Its impact will create a tidal wave, destroying one-third of the world's ships.

**sea became blood** (v. 8)—This may refer to an event known as red tides, caused by billions of dead micro-organisms poisoning the water—in this case the result of the meteor's collision. Or it may be actual blood, a clear act of eschatological judgment.

**great star fell** (v. 10)—Another celestial body, perhaps a comet in this case since it leaves a fiery trail (see v. 8; 6:13); it will disintegrate as it nears the earth, scattering over the globe.

**Wormwood** (v. 11)—a bitter, poisonous substance, derived from a root, which causes drunkenness and eventually death (Prov. 5:4; Jer. 9:15)

**a third of the sun was struck** (v. 12)—God will supernaturally reduce the intensity of the celestial bodies by one-third. The loss of solar heat will cause a radical drop in temperature, producing severe changes in meteorological, botanical, and biological cycles; but this is temporary (see 16:8–9).

**Woe, woe, woe** (v. 13)—one for each remaining trumpet blast; although the first four trumpets are unimaginable, they will be nothing like the three to come (9:1–21; 11:15–19)

**a star fallen from heaven** (9:1)—Unlike the other stars that will have fallen (6:13; 8:8), this one will be an angelic being (see v. 2)—probably Satan himself (v. 4; 12:7).

**bottomless pit** (v. 1)—literally "pit of the abyss"; mentioned seven times in Revelation, it always refers to the prison where some of the demonic hordes are incarcerated, the place of severest torment and isolation (vv. 1–2, 11; 11:7; 17:8; 20:1, 3)

**locusts** (v. 3)—Grasshopper-like insects that descend in swarms so thick they can obscure the sun and strip bare all vegetation. In the 1950s a locust swarm devoured every growing thing for several hundred thousand square miles in the Middle East. These are not normal locusts, however, but specially prepared ones that are merely the outward form of demons, who, like locusts, will bring swarming desolation. "Like" appears nine times in John's description; he finds it difficult to describe what he sees in a way the reader can understand.

**scorpions** (v. 3)—This arachnid inhabits warm, dry regions and has an erect tail tipped with a venomous stinger. A scorpion's victim often rolls on the ground

the stars, so that a third of them were darkened. A third of the day did not shine, and likewise the night.

**13** *And I looked, and I heard an angel flying through the midst of heaven, saying with a loud voice, "Woe, woe, woe to the inhabitants of the earth, because of the remaining blasts of the trumpet of the three angels who are about to sound!"*

**9:1** *Then the fifth angel sounded: And I saw a star fallen from heaven to the earth. To him was given the key to the bottomless pit.*

**2** *And he opened the bottomless pit, and smoke arose out of the pit like the smoke of a great furnace. So the sun and the air were darkened because of the smoke of the pit.*

**3** *Then out of the smoke locusts came upon the earth. And to them was given power, as the scorpions of the earth have power.*

**4** *They were commanded not to harm the grass of the earth, or any green thing, or any tree, but only those men who do not have the seal of God on their foreheads.*

**5** *And they were not given authority to kill them, but to torment them for five months. Their torment was like the torment of a scorpion when it strikes a man.*

**6** *In those days men will seek death and will not find it; they will desire to die, and death will flee from them.*

**7** *The shape of the locusts was like horses prepared for battle. On their heads were crowns of something like gold, and their faces were like the faces of men.*

in agony, foams at the mouth, and grinds his teeth in pain. The demons in locust form are able to inflict physical—and perhaps, spiritual—pain like the scorpion (v. 5).

**men who do not have the seal of God** (v. 4)—everyone on earth except the two groups mentioned in chapter seven—the 144,000 Jewish evangelists and their converts (see 7:3)

**five months** (v. 5)—The normal life cycle of locusts is five months, usually from May to September.

**seek death and will not find it** (v. 6)—The tormented will find no relief. Even their unimaginable attempts to end their misery in suicide will be unsuccessful.

**faces of men** (v. 7)—probably a reference to these demonic creatures as rational, intelligent beings

8 *They had hair like women's hair, and their teeth were like lions' teeth.*

9 *And they had breastplates like breastplates of iron, and the sound of their wings was like the sound of chariots with many horses running into battle.*

10 *They had tails like scorpions, and there were stings in their tails. Their power was to hurt men five months.*

11 *And they had as king over them the angel of the bottomless pit, whose name in Hebrew is Abaddon, but in Greek he has the name Apollyon.*

12 *One woe is past. Behold, still two more woes are coming after these things.*

13 *Then the sixth angel sounded: And I heard a voice from the four horns of the golden altar which is before God,*

14 *saying to the sixth angel who had the trumpet, "Release the four angels who are bound at the great river Euphrates."*

15 *So the four angels, who had been prepared for the hour and day and month and year, were released to kill a third of mankind.*

16 *Now the number of the army of the horsemen was two hundred million; I heard the number of them.*

17 *And thus I saw the horses in the vision: those who sat on them had breastplates of fiery red, hyacinth blue, and sulfur yellow; and the heads of the horses were like the heads of lions; and out of their mouths came fire, smoke, and brimstone.*

**women's hair** (v. 8)—Jeremiah 51:27 refers to locusts having bristles like hair.

**lions' teeth** (v. 8)—They are fierce, powerful, and deadly.

**breastplates of iron** (v. 9)—Breastplates were designed to protect the vital organs and sustain the life of the warrior. These creatures are invulnerable.

**Abaddon . . . Apollyon** (v. 11)—Although locusts normally have no king (Prov. 30:27), these demonic creatures do. His name in both Hebrew and Greek means "destroyer." There is a hierarchy of power among the demons, just as among the holy angels. Apparently, "the angel of the bottomless pit" is one of Satan's most trusted leaders.

**One woe** (v. 12)—the first of the final three trumpets (see 8:13)

**horns of the golden altar** (v. 13)—God's design for the golden altar of incense included small protrusions (horns) on each corner (see 6:9). Normally a place of mercy, as God responded to His people's prayers, the altar will resound with a cry for vengeance.

**four angels** (v. 14)—Scripture never refers to holy angels as being bound. These are fallen angels—another segment of Satan's force whom God had bound but who He will free to accomplish His judgment through their horsemen (vv. 15–19). God's control extends even to the demonic forces—they are bound or freed at His command.

**Euphrates** (v. 14)—This refers to one of the four rivers that flowed through the Garden of Eden (see 16:12). Starting with Babel, this region has spawned many of the world's pagan religions.

**the hour and day and month and year** (v. 15)—God works according to His predetermined plan.

**the army** (v. 16)—Some see this as a reference to forces accompanying the kings of the east (16:12) and identify them with a human army coming from Asia. But that event occurs in connection with the seventh trumpet, not the sixth. The language is better understood as referring to a demon force that makes war with the earth's inhabitants and kills one-third of humanity (v. 15).

**brimstone** (v. 17)—Brimstone is a yellowish, sulfuric rock that often attends fire and smoke in Revelation (14:10; 19:20; 20:10). Common in the Dead Sea region, these deposits melt when ignited and produce burning streams and suffocating gas.

*tails are like serpents, having heads* (v. 19)—John's language represents the demons' ability to vent their destructive power in both directions.

*demons* (v. 20)—reminiscent of Paul's comments about idolatry; demons impersonate the stone and wood idols men make

*sorceries* (v. 21)—This Greek word is the root of the English word "pharmacy." Drugs in the ancient world were used to dull the senses and induce a state suitable for religious experiences such as seances, witchcraft, incantations, and cavorting with mediums (21:8; 22:15).

18 By these three plagues a third of mankind was killed—by the fire and the smoke and the brimstone which came out of their mouths.

19 For their power is in their mouth and in their tails; for their tails are like serpents, having heads; and with them they do harm.

20 But the rest of mankind, who were not killed by these plagues, did not repent of the works of their hands, that they should not worship demons, and idols of gold, silver, brass, stone, and wood, which can neither see nor hear nor walk.

21 And they did not repent of their murders or their sorceries or their sexual immorality or their thefts.

1) What events unfold with the breaking of the seventh seal (8:1–5)?

_____

_____

_____

_____

_____

2) What is the meaning of the angel standing at the altar, holding the golden censer?

_____

_____

_____

_____

3) What will happen to the earth as a result of the first four trumpet judgments?

_____

_____

_____

_____

4) Some have described the result of the sounding of the fifth trumpet (9:1–12) as "hell on earth." Why? What will happen when this event unfolds?

_____

_____

_____

_____

5) How do you explain the response of those who are left after the sixth trumpet's horrible judgment (9:13–21)?

_____

_____

_____

_____

## GOING DEEPER

The Old Testament prophets foresaw a mighty "Day of the Lord." For more insight, read Isaiah 13:1–13.

1  *The burden against Babylon which Isaiah the son of Amoz saw.*
2  *"Lift up a banner on the high mountain, raise your voice to them; wave your hand, that they may enter the gates of the nobles.*
3  *I have commanded My sanctified ones; I have also called My mighty ones for My anger—those who rejoice in My exaltation."*
4  *The noise of a multitude in the mountains, like that of many people! A tumultuous noise of the kingdoms of nations gathered together! The LORD of hosts musters the army for battle.*
5  *They come from a far country, from the end of heaven—the LORD and His weapons of indignation, to destroy the whole land.*
6  *Wail, for the day of the LORD is at hand! It will come as destruction from the Almighty.*
7  *Therefore all hands will be limp, every man's heart will melt,*
8  *And they will be afraid. Pangs and sorrows will take hold of them; they will be in pain as a woman in childbirth; they will be amazed at one another; their faces will be like flames.*
9  *Behold, the day of the LORD comes, cruel, with both wrath and fierce anger, to lay the land desolate; and He will destroy its sinners from it.*
10 *For the stars of heaven and their constellations will not give their light; the*

sun will be darkened in its going forth, and the moon will not cause its
light to shine.

11 "I will punish the world for its evil, and the wicked for their iniquity; I will
halt the arrogance of the proud, and will lay low the haughtiness of the
terrible.

12 I will make a mortal more rare than fine gold, a man more than the
golden wedge of Ophir.

13 Therefore I will shake the heavens, and the earth will move out of her
place, in the wrath of the LORD of hosts and in the day of His fierce anger.

## EXPLORING THE MEANING

6) What added insights does this Old Testament passage provide
concerning the Day of the Lord?

_____

_____

_____

_____

_____

7) Why will God judge the earth?

_____

_____

_____

_____

_____

8) Read Luke 10:18. How does this verse help you identify the "star fallen
from heaven" in Revelation 9:1?

_____

_____

_____

_____

*(Verses to consider: Isa. 14:12–15; Ezek. 28:12–16)*

9) Read 2 Peter 2:4. Who are the creatures incarcerated in the bottomless pit (Rev. 9:1–2)? Why is Satan's unlocking of this abyss such a horrible event?

_____

_____

_____

_____

_____

## Truth for Today

There is a sense in which the present age is man's day; he is free to do what he wants within certain limitations. It is also Satan's day, during which the "god of this age" (2 Cor. 4:4) has been granted certain liberties within the parameters of God's purposeful, sovereign tolerance. But God will not permit the present state of affairs to continue forever. He will end man's day, overthrow the usurper Satan, destroy the present evil world system, and establish the earthly kingdom of the Lord Jesus Christ. That future time of judgment is known, appropriately, as the Day of the Lord. That day involves a complete renovation of the universe and the earth by judgment and restoration.

## Reflecting on the Text

10) How has your view of God been altered or sharpened by this study?

_____

_____

_____

_____

_____

11) How has your view of Satan and his evils been shaped or modified by the truths of this lesson?

_____

_____

_____

_____

12) What does a healthy fear of God look like? In what areas of your life do you fail to revere God and treat Him as holy?

_____

_____

_____

_____

_____

## PERSONAL RESPONSE

Write out additional reflections, questions you may have, or a prayer.

_____

_____

_____

_____

_____

_____

_____

_____

_____

_____

_____

_____

_____

_____

_____

_____

# 7

# THE TWO WITNESSES
*Revelation 10:1–11:19*

## DRAWING NEAR

A friend asks you, "If God is so good, why is there so much evil in the world?" How do you respond?

_____

_____

_____

These chapters remind us that God is sovereign and that all events (past, present, and future) are under His control. How does this truth encourage you?

_____

_____

## THE CONTEXT

Throughout history, God's people have wondered why God has allowed evil in the world. The wicked often appear to prosper. Sin seemingly runs wild and unchecked. Why, people ask, does God not stop all the carnage, corruption, and chaos in the world? Why does He allow His children to suffer? When will divine justice prevail and the righteous be delivered and the wicked punished?

All the pain, sorrow, suffering, and evil in the world cause the godly to long for God to intervene. A day is coming when He *will* break His silence, a day when all the purposes of God concerning men and the world will be consummated. At this time, the Lord Jesus Christ will return and establish His earthly kingdom. The sounding of the seventh trumpet, which heralds the imminent return and reign of Christ, will usher in that long-anticipated day.

But before that seventh trumpet sounds there will be an interlude, described in 10:1–11:14. This pause gives John and his readers the occasion to assimilate the startling truths that have just been revealed. It also serves to encourage God's people in the midst of the fury and horror of divine judgment, reminding them that God is still sovereign. During the interlude, God comforts His people with the assurance that He has not forgotten them and that they will ultimately be victorious. The sounding of the seventh trumpet marks the end of this interlude and results in the seven rapid-fire catastrophic bowl judgments described later in chapters 15 and 16.

## Keys to the Text

*Two Witnesses:* These are individuals granted special power and authority by God to preach a message of judgment and salvation during the second half of the Tribulation. Fulfilling the Old Testament requirement of two or more witnesses to confirm testimony (see Deut. 19:15; John 8:17; Heb. 10:28), these two prophets will represent the culmination of God's testimony to Israel: a two-pronged message of His judgment and His gracious offer of the gospel to all who will repent and believe. While it is impossible to be dogmatic about the identity of these two witnesses, several observations suggest they might be Moses and Elijah: (1) like Moses, they strike the earth with plagues, and like Elijah, they have the power to keep it from raining; (2) Jewish tradition expected both Moses and Elijah to return in the future; (3) both Moses and Elijah were present at the Transfiguration, the preview of Christ's second coming; (4) both Moses and Elijah used supernatural means to provoke repentance; (5) Elijah was taken up alive into heaven, and God buried Moses' body where it would never be found; and (6) the length of the drought the two witnesses bring (three-and-one-half-years; see 11:3, 6) is the same as that brought by Elijah.

## Unleashing the Text

Read 10:1–11:19, noting the key words and definitions next to the passage.

### Revelation 10:1–11:19 (NKJV)

*another mighty angel* (v. 1)—Many commentators understand this to be Jesus Christ. But the Greek word translated "another" means one of the same kind, that is, a created being. This is not one of the seven angels responsible for sounding the trumpets (8:2), but one of the highest ranking in heaven, filled with splendor, greatness, and strength (see 5:2; 8:3; 18:1).

1 *I saw still another mighty angel coming down from heaven, clothed with a cloud. And a rainbow was on his head, his face was like the sun, and his feet like pillars of fire.*

2 *He had a little book open in his hand. And he set his right foot on the sea and his left foot on the land,*

*rainbow* (v. 1)—See 4:3. Perhaps God included this to remind John that, even in judgment, He will always remember His Noahic Covenant and protect His own.

*feet like pillars of fire* (v. 1)—This angel's feet and legs indicate the firm resolve with which he will execute the Day of the Lord.

*little book* (v. 2)—The seven-sealed scroll that is the title deed to the earth (see 5:1) will be fully opened and all the final judgments made visible.

*right foot on the sea and his left foot on the land* (v. 2)—Although Satan has temporarily usurped the sea and the earth, this symbolic act demonstrates that all creation belongs to the Lord and He rules it with sovereign authority.

3  and cried with a loud voice, as when a lion roars. When he cried out, seven thunders uttered their voices.

4  Now when the seven thunders uttered their voices, I was about to write; but I heard a voice from heaven saying to me, "Seal up the things which the seven thunders uttered, and do not write them."

5  The angel whom I saw standing on the sea and on the land raised up his hand to heaven

6  and swore by Him who lives forever and ever, who created heaven and the things that are in it, the earth and the things that are in it, and the sea and the things that are in it, that there should be delay no longer,

7  but in the days of the sounding of the seventh angel, when he is about to sound, the mystery of God would be finished, as He declared to His servants the prophets.

8  Then the voice which I heard from heaven spoke to me again and said, "Go, take the little book which is open in the hand of the angel who stands on the sea and on the earth."

9  So I went to the angel and said to him, "Give me the little book." And he said to me, "Take and eat it; and it will make your stomach bitter, but it will be as sweet as honey in your mouth."

10  Then I took the little book out of the angel's hand and ate it, and it was as sweet as honey in my mouth. But when I had eaten it, my stomach became bitter.

11  And he said to me, "You must prophesy again about many peoples, nations, tongues, and kings."

**Seal up** (v. 4)—John was told he must conceal the message of the seven thunders until God's time (see 22:10).

**raised up his hand** (v. 5)—This Greek verb appears often in the technical sense of raising the hand to take an oath or a solemn vow. The hand is raised toward heaven because that is where God dwells. The angel is taking an oath.

**there should be delay no longer** (v. 6)—This initiates the last plagues of the Day of the Lord (11:15), indicating that the time the disciples anticipated has come. The prayers of the saints will be answered (6:9–11).

**the mystery** (v. 7)—This is a Greek term meaning "to shut" or "to close." In the New Testament, a "mystery" is a truth that God concealed but has revealed through Christ and His apostles. Here the mystery is the final consummation of all things as God destroys sinners and establishes His righteous kingdom on earth.

**as He declared** (v. 7)—This mystery, though not fully revealed, was declared to God's prophets.

**Take and eat it** (v. 9)—This act graphically illustrates taking in God's Word. John's physical reactions demonstrate what every believer's proper response to God's judgment should be—sweet anticipation of God's glory and our victory, and at the same time, the bitterness of seeing God's wrath poured out on those who reject His Son.

**your stomach bitter** (v. 9)—As he truly digests what the seal, trumpet, and bowl judgments hold in store for the sinner, John becomes nauseated.

**sweet as honey in your mouth** (v. 9)—But still God's final victory and vindication are sweet realities to the believer.

**prophesy again** (v. 11)—a call for John to warn men about the bitter judgment in the seventh trumpet and the seven bowls

**a reed** (11:1)—This refers to a hollow, bamboo-like cane plant that grew in the Jordan Valley. Because of its light weight and rigidity, it was commonly used as a measuring rod. Measuring the temple signified God's ownership of it (see 21:15).

**the temple of God** (v. 1)—refers to the Holy of Holies and the Most Holy Place, not the entire temple complex (see v. 2); a rebuilt temple will exist during the time of the Tribulation

**altar** (v. 1)—The reference to worshipers suggests this is the bronze altar in the courtyard, not the incense altar in the Most Holy Place, since only the priests were permitted inside the Most Holy Place.

**court which is outside** (v. 2)—This refers to the court of the Gentiles, separated from the inner court in the Herodian temple by a low wall. Gentiles were forbidden to enter the inner court on penalty of death. That John is instructed not to measure the outer court symbolizes God's rejection of the unbelieving Gentiles who have oppressed His covenant people.

**11:1** Then I was given a reed like a measuring rod. And the angel stood, saying, "Rise and measure the temple of God, the altar, and those who worship there.

2 But leave out the court which is outside the temple, and do not measure it, for it has been given to the Gentiles. And they will tread the holy city underfoot for forty-two months.

3 And I will give power to my two witnesses, and they will prophesy one thousand two hundred and sixty days, clothed in sackcloth."

4 These are the two olive trees and the two lampstands standing before the God of the earth.

5 And if anyone wants to harm them, fire proceeds from their mouth and devours their enemies. And if anyone wants to harm them, he must be killed in this manner.

6 These have power to shut heaven, so that no rain falls in the days of their prophecy; and they have

**tread the holy city underfoot** (v. 2)—Assyria, Babylon, Medo-Persia, Greece, and Rome all oppressed Jerusalem in ancient times (see 2 Kings 25:8–10; Ps. 79:1; Isa. 63:18; Lam. 1:10). This verse refers to the future devastating destruction and oppression of Jerusalem by the forces of the Antichrist.

**forty-two months** (v. 2)—This three-and-one-half-year period covers the second half of the Tribulation and coincides with the visibly evil career of the Antichrist (v. 3; 12:6; 13:5). During this same time, the Jews will be sheltered by God in the wilderness (12:6, 14).

**one thousand two hundred and sixty days** (v. 3)—forty-two months or three and one-half years (see 12:6; 13:5; see v. 2)

**sackcloth** (v. 3)—This was a coarse, rough cloth made from goat or camel hair. Wearing garments made from it expressed penitence, humility, and mourning (see 2 Sam. 3:31; 2 Kings 6:30; Esth. 4:1; Isa. 22:12; Jer. 6:26; Matt. 11:21). The witnesses are mourning because of the wretched wickedness of the world, God's judgment on it, and the desecration of the temple and the holy city by the Antichrist.

**two olive trees and the two lampstands** (v. 4)—Olive oil was commonly used in lamps; together the olive trees and lampstands symbolize the light of spiritual revival. The two witnesses' preaching will spark a revival, just as Joshua's and Zerubbabel's did in Israel after the Babylonian captivity.

**fire proceeds . . . and devours** (v. 5)—This probably refers to literal fire. These two will be invincible during their ministry, protected by supernatural power. The false prophet will counterfeit this sign (13:3).

**power to shut heaven** (v. 6)—Miracles have often authenticated God's messengers. The three-and-one-half-year drought they will bring (as Elijah did before them) will add immeasurable torment to those experiencing the worldwide disasters of the Tribulation and it will increase their hatred of the two witnesses.

power over waters to turn them to blood, and to strike the earth with all plagues, as often as they desire.

7 When they finish their testimony, the beast that ascends out of the bottomless pit will make war against them, overcome them, and kill them.

8 And their dead bodies will lie in the street of the great city which spiritually is called Sodom and Egypt, where also our Lord was crucified.

9 Then those from the peoples, tribes, tongues, and nations will see their dead bodies three-and-a-half days, and not allow their dead bodies to be put into graves.

10 And those who dwell on the earth will rejoice over them, make merry, and send gifts to one another, because these two prophets tormented those who dwell on the earth.

11 Now after the three-and-a-half days the breath of life from God entered them, and they stood on their feet, and great fear fell on those who saw them.

12 And they heard a loud voice from heaven saying to them, "Come up here." And they ascended to heaven in a cloud, and their enemies saw them.

13 In the same hour there was a great earthquake, and a tenth of the city fell. In the earthquake seven

**waters to turn them to blood** (v. 6)—The earth's water, already devastated by the effects of the second and third trumpets, will become undrinkable, adding immensely to the suffering caused by the drought.

**the beast** (v. 7)—The first of 36 references to this person in Revelation, who is none other than the Antichrist (see ch. 13). That he will ascend out of the bottomless pit indicates that his power is satanic.

**kill them** (v. 7)—Their ministry completed, God will withdraw the two witnesses' supernatural protection. The beast will then be able to accomplish what many had died trying to do.

**bodies will lie in the street** (v. 8)—Refusing to bury one's enemies was a way to dishonor and show contempt for them. The Old Testament expressly forbids this practice.

**the great city** (v. 8)—Identifying Jerusalem as a city like Sodom and Egypt stresses the city's wickedness. Its Jewish population will apparently be the focus of the witnesses' ministry, leading to the conversions of verse 13.

**three-and-a-half days** (v. 9)—The entire world will watch (undoubtedly on the latest form of visual media) and glorify the Antichrist as the bodies of the dead prophets who have been killed begin to decay.

**rejoice . . . make merry . . . send gifts** (v. 10)—Wild with joy over the death of their tormentors, those who dwell on the earth (a phrase used eleven times in Revelation to speak of unbelievers) will celebrate the two witnesses' deaths as a holiday.

**breath of life from God entered them** (v. 11)—The festivities, however, are short-lived as God vindicates His faithful witnesses by resurrecting them.

**ascended to heaven in a cloud** (v. 12)—Some may wonder why God will not allow them to preach, assuming their message would have more force following their resurrection. But that ignores Christ's clear statement to the contrary (Luke 16:31).

**enemies saw them** (v. 12)—Those who hated and dishonored the two witnesses will watch their vindication.

**earthquake** (v. 13)—God punctuates the ascension of His prophets with a shattering earthquake. The destruction and loss of life may be primarily among the leaders of the Antichrist's forces.

**the rest** (v. 13)—This refers to the Jews still living, who will not yet have come to faith in Christ.

**gave glory to the God of heaven** (v. 13)—a genuine experience of the salvation of Jews, in contrast to those who blaspheme and refuse to glorify God (16:9); this makes a key fulfillment of Zechariah's and Paul's prophecies (Zech. 12:10; 13:1; Rom. 11:25–27)

**second woe** (v. 14)—This refers to the sixth trumpet (see 9:12). The interlude between the sixth and seventh trumpets ends (see 10:1). Israel's repentance will shortly usher in the millennial kingdom (Acts 3:19–21; Rom. 11:25–26). But first will come the final, climactic judgments.

**seventh angel sounded** (v. 15)—The seventh trumpet includes the seven bowls, the final judgments depicted in chapter 16, and all the events leading up to the establishing of the millennial kingdom (ch. 20) and the coronation of Jesus as King (ch. 19).

thousand people were killed, and the rest were afraid and gave glory to the God of heaven.

14 The second woe is past. Behold, the third woe is coming quickly.

15 Then the seventh angel sounded: And there were loud voices in heaven, saying, "The kingdoms of this world have become the kingdoms of our Lord and of His Christ, and He shall reign forever and ever!"

16 And the twenty-four elders who sat before God on their thrones fell on their faces and worshiped God,

17 saying: "We give You thanks, O Lord God Almighty, the One who is and who was and who is to come, because You have taken Your great power and reigned.

18 The nations were angry, and Your wrath has come, and the time of the dead, that they should be judged, and that You should reward Your servants the prophets and the saints, and those who fear Your name, small and great, and should destroy those who destroy the earth."

**kingdoms of our Lord and of His Christ** (v. 15)—The singular ("kingdom") is the preferred reading. Despite its many political and cultural divisions, the Bible views the world spiritually as one kingdom, with one ruler—Satan (John 12:31). Following Satan's lead, the human rulers of this world are generally hostile to Christ (Ps. 2:2). The long rebellion of the world kingdom will end with the victorious return of the Lord Jesus Christ to defeat His enemies and establish His messianic kingdom (Dan. 2:44). This kingdom also belongs to God the Father (see Dan. 4:3; 6:26).

**One who is and who was** (v. 17)—The final phrase, "who is to come," (used in 1:4, 8; 4:8), is omitted in the most reliable Greek manuscripts. The coming of the kingdom is no longer future, but will be immediate.

**nations were angry** (v. 18)—No longer terrified (see 6:15–17), they will be filled with defiant rage. Their hostility will shortly manifest itself in a foolish attempt to fight against Christ—a doomed, futile effort that is the apex of human rebellion against God (16:14; 19:17–21).

**Your wrath** (v. 18)—Almighty God answers the feeble, impotent fury of the nations. The 24 elders speak of God's future wrath (20:11–15) as if it were already present, signifying its certainty. That God will one day pour out His wrath on rebellious men is a major theme in Scripture.

**dead . . . judged** (v. 18)—The final outpouring of God's wrath includes judging the dead (see Matt. 25:31–46; John 5:25–29). The judgment has two parts: (1) God rewards Old Testament saints (Dan. 12:1–3; see 22:12; 1 Cor. 3:8; 4:5), the raptured Church (1 Cor. 15:51–52; 1 Thess. 4:13–18), and Tribulation saints (20:4); and (2) God condemns unbelievers to the lake of fire forever (20:15).

**19** *Then the temple of God was opened in heaven, and the ark of His covenant was seen in His temple. And there were lightnings, noises, thunderings, an earthquake, and great hail.*

*temple of God . . . heaven* (v. 19)—See 3:12; 7:15; 14:15, 17; 15:5–8; 16:1, 17. The heavenly Holy of Holies (see Exod. 26:31–37) where God dwells in transcendent glory, is already identified as His throne (chs. 4–5). See Hebrews 9:24. John had seen the throne (4:5), the altar (6:9; 8:3–5), and now the Holy of Holies.

*ark of His covenant* (v. 19)—This piece of furniture in the Old Testament tabernacle and temple symbolized God's presence, atonement, and covenant with His people. That earthly ark was only a picture of this heavenly one (see Heb. 9:23). It was there God provided mercy and atonement for sin. As the earthly Holy of Holies was open when the price of sin was paid, so the Holy of Holies in heaven is opened to speak of God's saving New Covenant and redeeming purpose in the midst of judgment.

*lightnings, noises, thunderings, an earthquake, and great hail* (v. 19)—What was anticipated in 4:5 and 8:5 will become a terrifying reality. These events occur as part of the seventh bowl (16:17–21) and are the climax of the seventh trumpeter. Since heaven is the source of vengeance, judgment also comes out of God's Holy of Holies (14:15, 17; 15:5–8; 16:1, 7, 17; see 6:1).

1) In 10:1–2, John saw an angel come down from heaven. What happened next? What did the angel do? What was John commanded to do?

_____

_____

_____

_____

(*Verses to consider: Deut. 32:39–42; Ps. 19:7–11; 69:24; Jer. 15:16; 25:30*)

2) Why was John given a measuring rod and what did the angel tell him to do?

_____

_____

_____

3) Summarize the work of the two witnesses (11:1–14). What will result from their ministry?

_____

_____

_____

_____

4) What happened with the sounding of the seventh trumpet (11:15–19)?

_____

_____

_____

5) How does this passage demonstrate God's sovereignty?

_____

_____

_____

_____

## Going Deeper

The problem of evil is not new. King David encountered many enemies of God and saw evil men flourish. Read what he observed in Psalm 2:1–12.

1   *Why do the nations rage, and the people plot a vain thing?*
2   *The kings of the earth set themselves, and the rulers take counsel together, against the LORD and against His Anointed, saying,*
3   *"Let us break their bonds in pieces and cast away their cords from us."*
4   *He who sits in the heavens shall laugh; the LORD shall hold them in derision.*
5   *Then He shall speak to them in His wrath, and distress them in His deep displeasure:*
6   *"Yet I have set My King on My holy hill of Zion."*
7   *"I will declare the decree: The LORD has said to Me, 'You are My Son, today I have begotten You.*
8   *Ask of Me, and I will give You the nations for Your inheritance, and the ends of the earth for Your possession.*
9   *You shall break them with a rod of iron; You shall dash them to pieces like a potter's vessel.' "*
10   *Now therefore, be wise, O kings; be instructed, you judges of the earth.*
11   *Serve the LORD with fear, and rejoice with trembling.*
12   *Kiss the Son, lest He be angry, and you perish in the way, when His wrath is kindled but a little. Blessed are all those who put their trust in Him.*

## Exploring the Meaning

6) Describe the nations' attitude toward God. What is the psalmist's advice to them?

_____

_____

_____

7) Who is the "King of Zion" mentioned here (vv. 6–7)? What will he accomplish?

_____

_____

_____

8) In Revelation 11, we've seen how the two witnesses play a major role in the unfolding of events. Read Mark 9:1–10. Why do many commentators and Bible scholars believe that the two witnesses will be Moses and Elijah?

_____

_____

_____

_____

*(Verses to consider: Deut. 18:15–18; 34:5–6; 2 Kings 2:11; Mal. 4:5, 6; John 1:21; James 5:17)*

## Truth for Today

As an exile on the island of Patmos, John had no opportunity to preach to all nations. But John recorded these prophecies to warn all sinners that, while judgment is presently restrained, a future day is coming when the seventh angel will sound his trumpet and sin's dominion will be broken. In that day the freedom of Satan and his demons will come to an end, godless men will be judged, and believers will be glorified. These chapters present an interlude of hope tinged with bitterness that reminds all Christians of their evangelistic responsibilities to warn the world of that day.

## Reflecting on the Text

9) In his vision, John ate the "little book" and it was both bitter and sweet to him. In what ways is what you're studying bitter and sweet to you?

_____

_____

_____

_____

_____

10) John's calling to tell the world all that had been revealed to him is reminiscent of the Great Commission (Matt. 28:18–20). How passionate are you about sharing God's truth with family members, friends, neighbors, and coworkers? What keeps you from being a more active witness for Christ?

_____

_____

_____

_____

_____

## Personal Response

Write out additional reflections, questions you may have, or a prayer.

_____

_____

_____

_____

_____

_____

_____

_____

# 8

# THE TERRIBLE TRIUMVIRATE

*Revelation 12:1–13:18*

## DRAWING NEAR

How do the media and Hollywood films portray supernatural evil and demonic activity? Is this accurate according to the Bible's view?

_____

_____

_____

Have you ever been in a situation or around a person that seemed to epitomize "evil"? Describe your experience of coming "face-to-face" (either literally or figuratively) with such blatant, intense wickedness.

_____

_____

_____

What speculations have you heard about the identity of the Antichrist?

_____

_____

_____

_____

## THE CONTEXT

Our world is the theater where God's glorious story of redemption is played out. Satan and his demonic hosts have attacked the human race, turning the earth into the main battleground in their cosmic war against God, the holy angels, and the elect. This study focuses on the terrible three enemies to come: Satan (the dragon), Antichrist (the first beast), and the false prophet (the second beast). The beasts represent the final Antichrist, whose career spans the same time period as the seal and trumpet judgments.

In the future, Satan will serve God's purpose by being permitted to launch another deadly assault against the human race. That attack will take place during the Great Tribulation. He and his demonic forces will unsuccessfully battle Michael and the heavenly host (that is, the holy angels of God). As a result of their defeat, the devil and his demons will be permanently cast down to the earth. With his theater of operations then restricted and his time running out, Satan will marshal all of his malevolent, fallen angels in an all-out attempt to deceive and destroy the souls of men.

Chapters 12–14 are actually a digression in John's vision, taking readers back through the Tribulation from Satan's perspective. These chapters are filled with difficult apocalyptic imagery and symbolism. Take time to read the study notes next to the passage for further explanation and interpretation of these things.

## KEYS TO THE TEXT

*Satan:* The name *Satan*, meaning "adversary" or "enemy," appears especially in Job and the Gospels. The term *devil* comes from a Greek verb meaning "to slander" or "to falsely accuse." The Bible identifies him as a murderer, a liar, a roaring lion seeking to devour, the god of this evil age, the tempter, the dragon, the serpent, and the "accuser of the brethren" (Rev. 12:10). His accusations against believers are unsuccessful because Christ is our Advocate (1 John 2:1). The Lord provides His saints with sufficient armor to combat and thwart the adversary (Eph. 6). Ultimately, Satan's power over Christians is already broken and the war is won through Christ's crucifixion and resurrection, which forever conquered the power of sin and death.

*Antichrist:* A false prophet and evil being who will set himself up against Christ and the people of God in the last days before the second coming of Christ. Used only in the writings of John in the New Testament, the term refers to one who stands in opposition to all that Jesus Christ represents (1 John 2:18, 22; 4:3; 2 John 7). John wrote that several antichrists existed already in his day—false teachers who denied the deity and the incarnation of Christ—but that the supreme Antichrist of history would appear at some future time. Paul called him the "man of sin" and the "lawless one" (2 Thess. 2). This man is not Satan, although Satan is the force behind him. He exalts himself, declaring himself to be God and demanding the worship of the world. In this act of satanic self-deification, he defies God. Antichrist (the first beast) will be primarily a political and military leader, but the false prophet (second beast) will be a religious leader. Politics and religion will unite in a worldwide religion of worshiping the Antichrist (see Rev. 17:1–9, 15–17).

# Unleashing the Text

Read 12:1–13:18, noting the key words and definitions next to the passage.

## Revelation 12:1–13:18 (NKJV)

12:1 *Now a great sign appeared in heaven: a woman clothed with the sun, with the moon under her feet, and on her head a garland of twelve stars.*

2 *Then being with child, she cried out in labor and in pain to give birth.*

3 *And another sign appeared in heaven: behold, a great, fiery red dragon having seven heads and ten horns, and seven diadems on his heads.*

4 *His tail drew a third of the stars of heaven and threw them to the earth. And the dragon stood before the woman who was ready to give birth, to devour her Child as soon as it was born.*

5 *She bore a male Child who was to rule all nations with a rod of iron. And her Child was caught up to God and His throne.*

**sign** (v. 1)—a symbol pointing to something else; this is the first of seven signs in the last half of Revelation (see v. 3; 13:13–14; 15:1; 16:14; 19:20)

**a woman** (v. 1)—This is not an actual woman, but a symbolic representation of Israel, pictured in the Old Testament as the wife of God (Hos. 2:16). Three other symbolic women appear in Revelation: (1) Jezebel, who represents paganism (2:20); (2) the scarlet woman (17:3–6), symbolizing the apostate church; and (3) the wife of the Lamb (19:7), symbolizing the true church. That this woman does not represent the church is clear from the context.

**clothed with the sun . . . moon under her feet . . . twelve stars** (v. 1)—Being clothed with the sun speaks of the glory, dignity, and exalted status of Israel, the people of promise who will be saved and given a kingdom. The picture of the moon under her feet possibly describes God's covenant relationship with Israel, since new moons were associated with worship (1 Chron. 23:31; 2 Chron. 2:4; 8:13; Ezra 3:5; Ps. 81:3). The twelve stars represent the twelve tribes of Israel.

**cried out . . . in pain** (v. 2)—Israel, often pictured as a mother giving birth (see Isa. 26:17–18; 54:1; 66:7–12), has agonized and suffered for centuries, longing for the Messiah to come and destroy Satan, sin, and death, and usher in the kingdom.

**great, fiery red dragon** (v. 3)—The woman's mortal enemy is Satan, who appears as a dragon thirteen times in this book (see v. 9; 20:2). Red speaks of bloodshed.

**seven heads . . . ten horns . . . seven diadems** (v. 3)—This figurative language depicts Satan's domination of seven past worldly kingdoms and ten future kingdoms. See 13:1; 17:9–10. Satan has ruled and will rule the world until the seventh trumpet blows (11:15). He has inflicted relentless pain on Israel, desiring to kill the woman before she could bring forth the child that would destroy him.

**a third of the stars of heaven** (v. 4)—Satan's original rebellion resulted in one-third of the angelic host joining his insurrection and becoming demons.

**to devour her Child** (v. 4)—Unable to prevent the virgin birth of Christ, Satan tried to kill the child in a general massacre of male children commanded by Herod.

**a male Child** (v. 5)—Jesus Christ in His incarnation was of Jewish descent. Despite Satan's efforts to destroy Israel and the messianic line, Jesus' birth took place as predicted by the prophets.

**rod of iron** (v. 5)—describes Jesus' coronation as King over the nations of the world (see 11:15; 19:15).

**her Child was caught up to God** (v. 5)—Christ's ascension is in view (Acts 1:9; Heb. 1:1–3).

**wilderness** (v. 6)—God will protect Israel from Satan by hiding her in the wilderness, perhaps in the region of Moab, Ammon, and Edom, east of Palestine. Interestingly, those countries will be specifically spared from the Antichrist's attack against the Holy Land (see Dan. 11:41).

**one thousand two hundred and sixty days** (v. 6)—At the midpoint of the Tribulation, the Antichrist breaks his covenant with Israel, puts a stop to temple worship, sets up the abomination of desolation (Dan. 9:27; Matt. 24:15), and devastates Jerusalem (11:2). At that time, many Jews flee for their lives (Matt. 24:16–22). God will preserve them during the last 1,260 days (forty-two months; three-and-one-half-years) constituting the Great Tribulation (see 3:10; 6:1, 9).

**war broke out in heaven** (v. 7)—The tumultuous events on earth during the Tribulation find their counter-part in heaven. A state of war has existed since the fall of Satan (see v. 4). Something will intensify that warfare—possibly the raptured saints passing through the realm of Satan.

**dragon was cast . . . to the earth** (v. 9)—Satan and his demons were cast out of heaven at the time of their original rebellion, but still have access to it. That access will then be denied, and they will be forever barred from heaven.

6 Then the woman fled into the wilderness, where she has a place prepared by God, that they should feed her there one thousand two hundred and sixty days.

7 And war broke out in heaven: Michael and his angels fought with the dragon; and the dragon and his angels fought,

8 but they did not prevail, nor was a place found for them in heaven any longer.

9 So the great dragon was cast out, that serpent of old, called the Devil and Satan, who deceives the whole world; he was cast to the earth, and his angels were cast out with him.

10 Then I heard a loud voice saying in heaven, "Now salvation, and strength, and the kingdom of our God, and the power of His Christ have come, for the accuser of our brethren, who accused them before our God day and night, has been cast down.

11 And they overcame him by the blood of the Lamb and by the word of their testimony, and they did not love their lives to the death.

12 Therefore rejoice, O heavens, and you who dwell in them! Woe to the inhabitants of the earth and the sea! For the devil has come down to you, having great wrath, because he knows that he has a short time."

13 Now when the dragon saw that he had been cast to the earth, he persecuted the woman who gave birth to the male Child.

**deceives the whole world** (v. 9)—As he has throughout human history, Satan will deceive people during the Tribulation (see 13:14; 20:3). After his temporary release from the bottomless pit at the end of the Millennium, he will briefly resume his deceitful ways (20:8, 10).

**accuser** (v. 10)—See verse 9. Satan will no longer accuse believers before the throne of God because he will no longer have access to heaven.

**blood of the Lamb** (v. 11)—No accusation can stand against those whose sins have been forgiven because of Christ's sacrificial death (see Rom. 8:33–39).

**he has a short time** (v. 12)—Knowing that his time is limited, Satan will intensify his efforts against God and mankind, and specifically target Israel (vv. 13, 17).

**14** But the woman was given two wings of a great eagle, that she might fly into the wilderness to her place, where she is nourished for a time and times and half a time, from the presence of the serpent.

**15** So the serpent spewed water out of his mouth like a flood after the woman, that he might cause her to be carried away by the flood.

**16** But the earth helped the woman, and the earth opened its mouth and swallowed up the flood which the dragon had spewed out of his mouth.

**17** And the dragon was enraged with the woman, and he went to make war with the rest of her offspring, who keep the commandments of God and have the testimony of Jesus Christ.

**13:1** Then I stood on the sand of the sea. And I saw a beast rising up out of the sea, having seven heads and ten horns, and on his horns ten crowns, and on his heads a blasphemous name.

**wings of a great eagle** (v. 14)—Not actual birds' wings, but a graphic depiction of God's providential protection of Israel. Wings often speak of protection. Eagles—probably vulture-like griffins—were the largest birds known in Palestine.

**a time and times and half a time** (v. 14)—Three-and-one-half-years; the second half of the Tribulation (see v. 6; 11:2–3; 13:5).

**earth opened its mouth** (v. 16)—A great army will come against Israel like a flood (v. 15), only to be swallowed up, perhaps in conjunction with one of the numerous earthquakes that occur during that period (6:12; 8:5; 11:13, 19; 16:18; Matt. 24:7).

**rest of her offspring** (v. 17)—Satan will turn his frustrated rage against every follower of the Lamb he can find—Jew or Gentile.

**commandments of God ... testimony of Jesus Christ** (v. 17)—The revealed truth from God and Christ contained in Scripture. Obedience to God's Word always marks a genuine believer.

**Then I stood** (13:1)—Most manuscripts read "He stood," referring again to the dragon, or Satan (see 12:9, 17). He takes a position in the midst of the nations of his world, represented by the sand of the sea.

**a beast** (v. 1)—Literally "a monster" (see 11:7), this describes a vicious, killing animal. In this context, the term represents both a person (Antichrist) and his system (the world). The final satanic world empire will be inseparable from the demon-possessed man who leads it.

**rising up out of the sea** (v. 1)—The sea represents the abyss or pit, the haunt of demons (see 11:7; 17:8; 20:1). The picture is of Satan summoning a powerful demon from the abyss, who then activates and controls the beast (Antichrist) and his empire.

**seven heads and ten horns** (v. 1)—This description is like that of Satan in 12:3. The heads may represent successive world empires—Egypt, Assyria, Babylon, Medo-Persia, Greece, Rome, and the final kingdom of Antichrist (see 17:9–10). The final one is made up of all the kingdoms represented by the horns (see notes for 17:12). Ten is a number that symbolizes the totality of human military and political power assisting the beast (Antichrist) as he controls the world. Horns always represent power, as in the animal kingdom—both offensive power (attack) and defensive power (protection). Daniel shows that the human Antichrist will rise up from these ten kings (Dan. 7:16–24). John picks up the numerical imagery of Daniel 2:41–42, which refers to the ten toes on the statue's clay and iron feet. The apostle sees the beast as the final world government—the anti-Christ, anti-God coalition—headed by a revived Roman Empire, having the strengths of various world powers, yet mixed with weakness and ultimately crushed (see Dan. 2:32–45; 7:7–8, 19–25; see 12:3). The crowns show the regal dominion of this confederate kingdom.

**blasphemous name** (v. 1)—Throughout history, every time a monarch has identified himself as a god, he has blasphemed the true God. Each ruler who contributes to the beast's final coalition has an identity, wears a crown, exerts dominion and power, and therefore blasphemes God.

**leopard** (v. 2)—This is a metaphor for ancient Greece, alluding to the Greeks' swiftness and agility as their military moved forward in conquest, particularly under Alexander the Great (see Dan. 7:6). The leopard and subsequent animal symbols were all native wildlife in Palestine, familiar to John's readers.

**bear** (v. 2)—a metaphor for the ancient Medo-Persian Empire, depicting that kingdom's ferocious strength, combined with its great stability (see Dan. 7:5)

**lion** (v. 2)—a metaphor for the ancient Babylonian Empire, referring to the Babylonians' fierce, all-consuming power as they extended their domain (see Dan. 7:4)

**his deadly wound was healed** (v. 3)—This statement could refer to one of the kingdoms that was destroyed and revived (that is, the Roman Empire). But more likely it refers to a fake death and resurrection enacted by the Antichrist, as part of his lying deception (see vv. 12, 14; 17:8, 11; 2 Thess. 2:9).

2 *Now the beast which I saw was like a leopard, his feet were like the feet of a bear, and his mouth like the mouth of a lion. The dragon gave him his power, his throne, and great authority.*

3 *And I saw one of his heads as if it had been mortally wounded, and his deadly wound was healed. And all the world marveled and followed the beast.*

4 *So they worshiped the dragon who gave authority to the beast; and they worshiped the beast, saying, "Who is like the beast? Who is able to make war with him?"*

5 *And he was given a mouth speaking great things and blasphemies, and he was given authority to continue for forty-two months.*

6 *Then he opened his mouth in blasphemy against God, to blaspheme His name, His tabernacle, and those who dwell in heaven.*

7 *It was granted to him to make war with the saints and to overcome them. And authority was given him over every tribe, tongue, and nation.*

8 *All who dwell on the earth will worship him, whose names have not been written in the Book of Life of the Lamb slain from the foundation of the world.*

**world marveled** (v. 3)—People in the world will be astounded and fascinated when the Antichrist appears to rise from the dead. His brilliance and attractive, but deluding, powers will cause the world to follow him unquestioningly (vv. 14; 2 Thess. 2:8–12).

**was given** (v. 5)—The sovereign God will establish the limits within which the Antichrist will be allowed to speak and operate. God will allow him to utter his blasphemies, to bring the rage of Satan to its culmination on earth for three-and-one-half-years (v. 5; 11:2–3; 12:6, 13–14).

**forty-two months** (v. 5)—This is the final three-and-one-half-years—1,260 days—of the "time of Jacob's trouble" (Jer. 30:7) and Daniel's seventieth week (Dan. 9:24–27), known as the Great Tribulation (see 11:2; 12:6; see Dan. 7:25). This last half is launched by the abomination of desolations (see Matt. 24:15).

**His name** (v. 6)—This identifies God and summarizes all His attributes.

**His tabernacle** (v. 6)—This is symbolic of heaven.

**those who dwell in heaven** (v. 6)—the angels and glorified saints who are before the throne of God and serve Him day and night

**make war with the saints** (v. 7)—The Antichrist will be allowed to massacre those who are God's children (see 6:9–11; 11:7; 17:14; see 17:6).

**Lamb slain** (v. 8)—The Lord Jesus who died to purchase the salvation of those whom God had chosen was fulfilling an eternal plan.

9 *If anyone has an ear, let him hear.*

10 *He who leads into captivity shall go into captivity; he who kills with the sword must be killed with the sword. Here is the patience and the faith of the saints.*

11 *Then I saw another beast coming up out of the earth, and he had two horns like a lamb and spoke like a dragon.*

12 *And he exercises all the authority of the first beast in his presence, and causes the earth and those who dwell in it to worship the first beast, whose deadly wound was healed.*

13 *He performs great signs, so that he even makes fire come down from heaven on the earth in the sight of men.*

**from the foundation of the world** (v. 8)—According to God's eternal, electing purpose before creation, the death of Christ seals the redemption of the elect forever (see Acts 2:23; 4:27–28). Antichrist can never take away the salvation of the elect. The eternal registry of the elect will never be altered, nor will truly saved people worship the Antichrist in the days of his rule.

**another beast** (v. 11)—This is the final false prophet (called such in 16:13; 19:20; 20:10) who promotes Antichrist's power and convinces the world to worship him as God. This companion beast will be the chief, most persuasive proponent of satanic religion (see 16:13; 19:20; 20:10). Antichrist will be primarily a political and military leader, but the false prophet will be a religious leader. Politics and religion will unite in a worldwide religion of worshiping the Antichrist (see 17:1–9, 15–17).

**out of the earth** (v. 11)—This is likely another reference to the abyss that lies below the earth. The false prophet will be sent forth and controlled by a powerful demon from below. The earth imagery, in contrast to that of the foreboding, mysterious sea in verse 1, may imply that the false prophet is subtler and more winsome than the Antichrist.

**two horns like a lamb** (v. 11)—This describes the relative weakness of the false prophet compared to Antichrist, who has ten horns. A lamb has only two small bumps on its head, very inferior to the ten-horned beast.

**like a lamb** (v. 11)—The lamb imagery may also imply that the false prophet will be a false Christ masquerading as the true Lamb. Unlike Antichrist, the false prophet will come not as a killing, destroying animal, but as one who appears gentle and deceptively attractive.

**spoke like a dragon** (v. 11)—The false prophet will be Satan's mouthpiece and thus his message will be like the dragon, Satan—the source of all false religion.

**exercises all the authority of the first beast** (v. 12)—The false prophet exercises the same kind of satanic power as Antichrist because he is empowered by the same source. He, too, will have worldwide influence and reputation as a miracle worker and speaker.

**causes . . . to worship** (v. 12)—"He causes" is used eight times of him. He wields influence to establish a false world religion headed by Antichrist and to entice people to accept that system.

**whose deadly wound was healed** (v. 12)—See v. 3; 17:8. This likely refers to the carefully crafted deception of a false resurrection after a false murder to inspire allegiance from the world.

**great signs** (v. 13)—The same phrase is used of Jesus' miracles (John 6:2), which indicates the false prophet performs signs that counterfeit Christ's. Satan, who has done supernatural works in the past (for example, Exod. 7:11), must use his strategy of false miracles to convince the world that Antichrist is more powerful than God's true witnesses (ch. 11), including Jesus Christ.

**fire come down from heaven** (v. 13)—The context indicates that the false prophet continually does counterfeit pyrotechnic signs in order to convince men of his power, and also in imitation of the two witnesses (11:5).

**make an image** (v. 14)—This refers to replication of Antichrist that is related to the throne he will erect during the abomination of desolation, halfway into the Tribulation period. This will happen in the Jerusalem temple when Antichrist abolishes the former false world religion and seeks to have people worship him alone as God. The false prophet and Antichrist will again deceive the world with a clever imitation of Christ, who will later return and reign from the true throne in Jerusalem.

**speak** (v. 15)—The false prophet will give the image of Antichrist the appearance of life, and the image will seem to utter words—contrary to what is normally true of idols (see Ps. 135:15, 16; Hab. 2:19).

**cause . . . to be killed** (v. 15)—His gentleness is a lie, since he is a killer (7:9–17). Some Gentiles will be spared to populate the kingdom (Matt. 25:31–40) and Jews will be protected (12:17).

14 *And he deceives those who dwell on the earth— by those signs which he was granted to do in the sight of the beast, telling those who dwell on the earth to make an image to the beast who was wounded by the sword and lived.*

15 *He was granted power to give breath to the image of the beast, that the image of the beast should both speak and cause as many as would not worship the image of the beast to be killed.*

16 *He causes all, both small and great, rich and poor, free and slave, to receive a mark on their right hand or on their foreheads,*

17 *and that no one may buy or sell except one who has the mark or the name of the beast, or the number of his name.*

18 *Here is wisdom. Let him who has understanding calculate the number of the beast, for it is the number of a man: His number is 666.*

**a mark** (v. 16)—In the Roman Empire, this was a normal identifying symbol, or brand, that slaves and soldiers bore on their bodies. Some of the ancient mystical cults delighted in such tattoos, which identified members with a form of worship. Antichrist will have a similar requirement, one that will need to be visible on the hand or forehead.

**buy or sell** (v. 17)—Antichrist's mark will allow people to engage in daily commerce, including the purchase of food and other necessities. Without the identifying mark, individuals will be cut off from the necessities of life.

**number of his name** (v. 17)—The beast (Antichrist) will have a name inherent in a numbering system. It is not clear from the text exactly what this name and number system will be or what its significance will be.

**His number is** (v. 18)—This is the essential number of a man. The number six falls one short of God's perfect number, seven, and thus represents human imperfection. Antichrist, the most powerful human the world will ever know, will still be a man, that is, a six. The ultimate in human and demonic power is a six, not perfect, as God is. The threefold repetition of the number is intended to reiterate and underscore man's identity. When Antichrist is finally revealed, there will be some way to identify him with this basic number of a man, or his name may have the numerical equivalent of 666. (In many languages, including Hebrew, Greek, and Latin, letters have numerical equivalents.) Because this text reveals very little about the meaning of 666, it is unwise to speculate beyond what is said.

1) The main characters described by John in chapter 12 are a woman, a male Child, and a dragon. Who or what is signified by each of these characters?

_____

_____

_____

_____

_____

2) Describe the cosmic conflict recorded in chapter 12. What was/is the outcome?

_____

_____

_____

_____

_____

*(Verses to consider: Job 1:6; 2:1; Dan. 10:13; Eph. 2:2; 6:10–19; Jude 9)*

3) What will happen to Israel during the Tribulation?

_____

_____

_____

_____

*(Verses to consider: Exod. 19:4; Deut. 32:9–12; Ps. 91:4; Isa. 40:31)*

4) What did John see in chapter 13? What did these characters do?

_____

_____

_____

_____

*(Verses to consider: Dan. 8:23–25; 9:24–27; 11:36–45; 2 Thess. 2:3–11).*

5) How is the second beast described (13:11)? How is he related to the first beast?

_____

_____

_____

_____

6) What is the "image" made by the beast (13:14)?

_____

_____

_____

*(Verses to consider: Dan. 9:27; 11:31; 12:11; Matt. 24:15; 2 Thess. 2:4)*

7) Why is the mark of the beast significant during the end times (13:16)?

_____

_____

_____

_____

## GOING DEEPER

Daniel's visions and prophecies of the end times contain similar imagery. Compare this Old Testament vision with Revelation. Read Daniel 7:1–28.

1 *In the first year of Belshazzar king of Babylon, Daniel had a dream and visions of his head while on his bed. Then he wrote down the dream, telling the main facts.*

2 *Daniel spoke, saying, "I saw in my vision by night, and behold, the four winds of heaven were stirring up the Great Sea.*

3 *And four great beasts came up from the sea, each different from the other.*

4 *The first was like a lion, and had eagle's wings. I watched till its wings were plucked off; and it was lifted up from the earth and made to stand on two feet like a man, and a man's heart was given to it.*

5 *"And suddenly another beast, a second, like a bear. It was raised up on one side, and had three ribs in its mouth between its teeth. And they said thus to it: 'Arise, devour much flesh!'*

6   "After this I looked, and there was another, like a leopard, which had on its back four wings of a bird. The beast also had four heads, and dominion was given to it.

7   "After this I saw in the night visions, and behold, a fourth beast, dreadful and terrible, exceedingly strong. It had huge iron teeth; it was devouring, breaking in pieces, and trampling the residue with its feet. It was different from all the beasts that were before it, and it had ten horns.

8   I was considering the horns, and there was another horn, a little one, coming up among them, before whom three of the first horns were plucked out by the roots. And there, in this horn, were eyes like the eyes of a man, and a mouth speaking pompous words.

9   "I watched till thrones were put in place, and the Ancient of Days was seated; His garment was white as snow, and the hair of His head was like pure wool. His throne was a fiery flame, its wheels a burning fire;

10   A fiery stream issued and came forth from before Him. A thousand thousands ministered to Him; ten thousand times ten thousand stood before Him. The court was seated, and the books were opened.

11   "I watched then because of the sound of the pompous words which the horn was speaking; I watched till the beast was slain, and its body destroyed and given to the burning flame.

12   As for the rest of the beasts, they had their dominion taken away, yet their lives were prolonged for a season and a time.

13   "I was watching in the night visions, and behold, One like the Son of Man, coming with the clouds of heaven! He came to the Ancient of Days, and they brought Him near before Him.

14   Then to Him was given dominion and glory and a kingdom, that all peoples, nations, and languages should serve Him. His dominion is an everlasting dominion, which shall not pass away, and His kingdom the one which shall not be destroyed.

15   "I, Daniel, was grieved in my spirit within my body, and the visions of my head troubled me.

16   I came near to one of those who stood by, and asked him the truth of all this. So he told me and made known to me the interpretation of these things:

17   'Those great beasts, which are four, are four kings which arise out of the earth.

18   But the saints of the Most High shall receive the kingdom, and possess the kingdom forever, even forever and ever.'

19   "Then I wished to know the truth about the fourth beast, which was different from all the others, exceedingly dreadful, with its teeth of iron

*and its nails of bronze, which devoured, broke in pieces, and trampled the residue with its feet;*

20 *and the ten horns that were on its head, and the other horn which came up, before which three fell, namely, that horn which had eyes and a mouth which spoke pompous words, whose appearance was greater than his fellows.*

21 *"I was watching; and the same horn was making war against the saints, and prevailing against them,*

22 *until the Ancient of Days came, and a judgment was made in favor of the saints of the Most High, and the time came for the saints to possess the kingdom.*

23 *"Thus he said: 'The fourth beast shall be a fourth kingdom on earth, which shall be different from all other kingdoms, and shall devour the whole earth, trample it and break it in pieces.*

24 *The ten horns are ten kings who shall arise from this kingdom. And another shall rise after them; he shall be different from the first ones, and shall subdue three kings.*

25 *He shall speak pompous words against the Most High, shall persecute the saints of the Most High, and shall intend to change times and law. Then the saints shall be given into his hand for a time and times and half a time.*

26 *'But the court shall be seated, and they shall take away his dominion, to consume and destroy it forever.*

27 *Then the kingdom and dominion, and the greatness of the kingdoms under the whole heaven, shall be given to the people, the saints of the Most High. His kingdom is an everlasting kingdom, and all dominions shall serve and obey Him.'*

28 *"This is the end of the account. As for me, Daniel, my thoughts greatly troubled me, and my countenance changed; but I kept the matter in my heart."*

## EXPLORING THE MEANING

8) What added insights does this passage contribute to your understanding of the beasts in Revelation 12–13?

_____

_____

_____

9) What promises are given of God's ultimate victory (vv. 9–14, 18, 22, 27)?

_____

_____

_____

_____

10) Read John 8:44. How did Jesus describe Satan?

_____

_____

_____

_____

*(Verses to consider: John 10:10; 1 Pet. 5:8; 1 John 3:8)*

## TRUTH FOR TODAY

The book of Revelation is the ultimate action thriller. Anyone who loves books filled with adventure and excitement will certainly love this book. The amazing Revelation contains drama, suspense, mystery, passion, and horror. It tells of apostasy by the church. It speaks of unprecedented economic collapse, and of the ultimate war of human history—the war that will truly end all wars. It describes natural disasters rivaled in intensity only by the world-wide Flood of Noah's day, as God will pour out His wrath on the sin-cursed earth. It speaks of the political intrigues that will lead to the ascendancy of the most evil and powerful dictator the world has ever known. Finally, and most terrifying of all, it describes the final judgment and the sentencing of all rebels, angelic and human, to eternal torment in hell. The book of Revelation is thus a book of astounding drama, horror, and pathos. Yet, amazingly, it is also a book of hope and joy with a happy ending, as sin, sorrow, and death are forever banished.

## REFLECTING ON THE TEXT

11) Should the reality of Satan and his evil intent alter the way you approach each day? If so, in what ways? If not, why not?

_____

_____

_____

12) Given the fact that Satan is a sworn enemy of God and His servants, how can you practically and specifically better support your pastor and church leaders this week?

_____

_____

_____

_____

13) What insight or truth from this lesson do you find most meaningful (i.e., comforting or convicting)?

_____

_____

_____

_____

## PERSONAL RESPONSE

Write out additional reflections, questions you may have, or a prayer.

_____

_____

_____

_____

_____

_____

_____

_____

_____

_____

_____

_____

# 9

# VICTORIOUS VOICES!

*Revelation 14:1–16:21*

## DRAWING NEAR

Think back over what you have studied thus far in the book of Revelation. What main themes have you seen over and over again?

_____

_____

_____

_____

Armageddon has become a somewhat overused symbol for fierce conflict, or even to describe football games and wrestling matches. What do you know about the Battle of Armageddon? What questions do you have?

_____

_____

_____

## THE CONTEXT

Revelation 14 serves as a preview of the end of the Great Tribulation. In this chapter, John shows his readers the triumph and vindication of the 144,000 faithful Israelites, who are redeemed by the blood of the Lamb. The fall of Babylon (symbolic of the Satanic world system) is foreseen and the fate of its loyalists foretold. The chapter then gives a summary glimpse of the battle of Armageddon, the great and terrible "winepress of the wrath of God."

Revelation 15 depicts the Tribulation saints who have overcome the beast. They sing songs of praise celebrating God's infinite power, perfect sovereignty, and eternal faithfulness. It also introduces the seven angels who are given the task of pouring out seven bowls of wrath, God's final judgments at the end of the seven-year Tribulation period. The bowl judgments are described in chapter 16 in rapid-fire staccato fashion, each one stronger in fury and intensity. Through all of this, the book of Revelation always reminds us that though the power of evil is great, God's plan and purposes will triumph and Jesus will be crowned King and Lord.

# Keys to the Text

*Song of Moses and Song of the Lamb:* The song of Moses was a song of victory sung by the people of Israel immediately after their crossing through the Red Sea (Exod. 15:1–21; see Deut. 32:1–43). The song of the Lamb refers to Christ's sacrificial death and extols God's powerful works in creation as He providentially upholds the universe. These two songs celebrate two great, redemptive events: (1) deliverance of Israel by God from Egypt through Moses; and (2) deliverance of sinners by God from sin through Christ. Like one gigantic choir, the redeemed of the Lord will sing and rejoice over the accomplishment of God's entire redemptive work before Christ's return.

*Seven Golden Bowls:* These bowls symbolize God's judgment. They are shallow saucers, familiar items often associated with various functions of the temple worship, such as serving wine or using in blood sacrifices. Their flat shallowness pictures how the divine judgments will be emptied instantly rather than slowly poured, drowning those who refused to drink the cup of salvation.

# Unleashing the Text

Read 14:1–16:21, noting the key words and definitions next to the passage.

## Revelation 14:1–16:21 (NKJV)

*Mount Zion* (14:1)—the city of Jerusalem, where Messiah will return and plant His feet

*name* (v. 1)—the counterpart to the mark of the beast; it is the stamp that will identify the 144,000 as belonging to God (see 13:6)

*new song* (v. 3)—This is the song of redemption, which is being sung by all the redeemed saints in one gigantic choir. They are rejoicing over the accomplishment of God's entire redemptive work before Christ's return.

*not defiled with women* (v. 4)—An illustration of God's ability to keep believers remarkably pure in the midst of great difficulty, this phrase indicates that the 144,000 Jewish evangelists will have not only resisted the perverse system of Antichrist but also will have resisted all temptations to illicit sex.

**14:1** Then I looked, and behold, a Lamb standing on Mount Zion, and with Him one hundred and forty-four thousand, having His Father's name written on their foreheads.

2 And I heard a voice from heaven, like the voice of many waters, and like the voice of loud thunder. And I heard the sound of harpists playing their harps.

3 They sang as it were a new song before the throne, before the four living creatures, and the elders; and no one could learn that song except the hundred and forty-four thousand who were redeemed from the earth.

4 These are the ones who were not defiled with women, for they are virgins. These are the ones

who follow the Lamb wherever He goes. These were redeemed from among men, being firstfruits to God and to the Lamb.

5 And in their mouth was found no deceit, for they are without fault before the throne of God.

6 Then I saw another angel flying in the midst of heaven, having the everlasting gospel to preach to those who dwell on the earth to every nation, tribe, tongue, and people—

7 saying with a loud voice, "Fear God and give glory to Him, for the hour of His judgment has come; and worship Him who made heaven and earth, the sea and springs of water."

8 And another angel followed, saying, "Babylon is fallen, is fallen, that great city, because she has made all nations drink of the wine of the wrath of her fornication."

**follow the Lamb** (v. 4)—This indicates partisanship for Jesus Christ. The victorious 144,000 are unwaveringly loyal to Him, whatever the cost.

**firstfruits** (v. 4)—Like the Old Testament firstfruits offering, these men will be set apart for special service to God (see Deut. 26:1–11). Some see firstfruits as the first large group of redeemed Israel (see 11:13), saved much earlier, and representative of more converts to follow (see Rom. 16:5; 1 Cor. 16:15), the firstfruits of a redeemed Israel (Rom. 11:1–5, 11–15, 25–27).

**no deceit** (v. 5)—The 144,000 speak God's truth accurately and precisely, with no exaggeration or understatement.

**without fault** (v. 5)—not sinless, but sanctified

**midst of heaven** (v. 6)—This is from a Greek term ("mid-heaven") denoting the point in the noonday sky where the sun reaches its zenith. This is the highest and brightest point, where all can see and hear.

**the everlasting gospel** (v. 6)—The angel is preaching the good news concerning everlasting life and entrance into the kingdom of God. He is urging the people of the world to change their allegiance from the beast to the Lamb. It is also called in the New Testament the gospel of God, the gospel of grace, the gospel of Christ, the gospel of peace, the glorious gospel, and the gospel of the kingdom. It is good news that God saves by the forgiveness of sin and opens His kingdom to all who will repent and believe. The whole world will hear this preaching by the angel as God graciously calls all to salvation.

**Fear God** (v. 7)—not Satan, nor Antichrist; this is the theme of Scripture, calling people to give honor, glory, worship, and reverence to God

**hour of His judgment has come** (v. 7)—The last moment arrives to repent and believe before God's wrath is poured out. This is the book's first use of the word *judgment*, a term that has the same meaning as *wrath* (see 6:17; 12:12).

**Him who made heaven and earth** (v. 7)—Creation is the great proof of God, which preachers will appeal to as the ground for all people to believe in Him and worship Him (see 4:11; 10:6; John 1:9; Acts 14:15–17; 17:23–28).

**Babylon is fallen** (v. 8)—Lack of response to the first angel's message causes a second angel to pronounce this judgment. *Babylon* refers to the entire worldwide political, economic, and religious kingdom of Antichrist (see 16:17–19 for details of this fall). The original city of Babylon was the birthplace of idolatry where the residents built the Tower of Babel, a monument to rebelliousness and false religion. Such idolatry was subsequently spread when God confounded humanity's language and scattered them around the world (see Gen. 11:1–9).

**wine of the wrath of her fornication** (v. 8)—This pictures Babylon causing the world to become intoxicated with her pleasures and enter an orgy of rebellion, hatred, and idolatry toward God. Fornication means spiritual prostitution to the Antichrist's false system.

**cup of His indignation** (v. 10)—Anyone loyal to the Antichrist and his kingdom will suffer the outpouring of God's collected wrath, done with the full force of His divine anger and unmitigated vengeance. Divine wrath is not an impulsive outburst of anger aimed capriciously at people God does not like. It is the settled, steady, merciless, graceless, and compassionless response of a righteous God against sin.

**fire and brimstone** (v. 10)—These are two elements that are often associated in Scripture with the torment of divine punishment. Here the reference is to hell, the lake of fire (see 19:20; 20:10; 21:8). Brimstone is a fiery sulfur (see 9:17).

**torment ascends forever and ever** (v. 11)—A reference to the eternality of hell (see Matt. 13:41–42; 25:41). Torment is the ceaseless infliction of unbearable pain, here prescribed for all who are loyal to Satan's leader.

**Son of Man** (v. 14)—The imagery of the Lord on a cloud emphasizes magnificent majesty (see 1:7; Matt. 24:30; 26:64).

**golden crown** (v. 14)—The victor's crown, a laurel wreath, was worn by those who celebrated victory in war or athletic competition. Christ now wears this particular crown, in this case made of gold, as a triumphant conqueror coming out of heaven to prevail over His enemies.

**sickle** (v. 14)—A harvesting tool with a razorsharp, curved steel or iron blade and a wooden handle, commonly used by ancient farmers to cut grain. It represents swift and devastating judgment.

**harvest of the earth** (v. 15)—The grain—in this case the ungodly people of the world—is ready to be gathered up and judged.

**temple** (v. 17)—See 11:19. This refers to the heavenly dwelling place of God, not the Tribulation temple in Jerusalem (see 11:1).

9 Then a third angel followed them, saying with a loud voice, "If anyone worships the beast and his image, and receives his mark on his forehead or on his hand,

10 he himself shall also drink of the wine of the wrath of God, which is poured out full strength into the cup of His indignation. He shall be tormented with fire and brimstone in the presence of the holy angels and in the presence of the Lamb.

11 And the smoke of their torment ascends forever and ever; and they have no rest day or night, who worship the beast and his image, and whoever receives the mark of his name."

12 Here is the patience of the saints; here are those who keep the commandments of God and the faith of Jesus.

13 Then I heard a voice from heaven saying to me, "Write: 'Blessed are the dead who die in the Lord from now on.' " "Yes," says the Spirit, "that they may rest from their labors, and their works follow them."

14 Then I looked, and behold, a white cloud, and on the cloud sat One like the Son of Man, having on His head a golden crown, and in His hand a sharp sickle.

15 And another angel came out of the temple, crying with a loud voice to Him who sat on the cloud, "Thrust in Your sickle and reap, for the time has come for You to reap, for the harvest of the earth is ripe."

16 So He who sat on the cloud thrust in His sickle on the earth, and the earth was reaped.

17 Then another angel came out of the temple which is in heaven, he also having a sharp sickle.

18 And another angel came out from the altar, who had power over fire, and he cried with a loud cry to him who had the sharp sickle, saying, "Thrust in your sharp sickle and gather the clusters of the vine of the earth, for her grapes are fully ripe."

19 So the angel thrust his sickle into the earth and gathered the vine of the earth, and threw it into the great winepress of the wrath of God.

20 And the winepress was trampled outside the city, and blood came out of the winepress, up to the horses' bridles, for one thousand six hundred furlongs.

15:1 Then I saw another sign in heaven, great and marvelous: seven angels having the seven last plagues, for in them the wrath of God is complete.

2 And I saw something like a sea of glass mingled with fire, and those who have the victory over the beast, over his image and over his mark and over the number of his name, standing on the sea of glass, having harps of God.

3 They sing the song of Moses, the servant of God, and

**another angel . . . who had power over fire** (v. 18)—This angel is associated with fire on the altar, which represents the prayers of the saints (6:9–11; 8:3–5). Fire refers to the constantly burning fire on the brass altar of the Jerusalem temple. Twice daily the priest would burn incense with that fire and offer the burning incense in the Most Holy Place as a symbol of the people's prayers (see 5:8; 6:9; 8:3). This angel is coming from the heavenly altar to ensure that all the prayers of all the saints for judgment and the coming of the kingdom are answered. He calls for judgment to start.

**winepress** (v. 19)—This vivid imagery signifies a horrendous slaughter or bloodbath. Here it refers to the slaughter of all the enemies of God who are still alive, facing the destruction at Armageddon, the final battle against God's enemies, staged on the Plain of Esdraelon. The bloody imagery comes from the fresh juice of stomped grapes splattering and running down a trough from the upper vat to the lower vat of a stone winepress.

**outside the city** (v. 20)—God will determine that this bloodbath will occur outside Jerusalem, as if God wants to protect the city from the carnage all around. Jerusalem will be attacked but will not be destroyed in the end, but spared for the glory of the kingdom, and the believing remnant will be saved as the Lord defends them and the city against the nations. They will escape through a newly created valley as the Lord finishes judgment and sets up His kingdom.

**up to the horses' bridles** (v. 20)—The severity of the slaughter is indicated in the imagery of the blood of those killed in the Battle of Armageddon splattering as high (about four feet) as the bridles of the horses involved. Equally likely, if the battle occurs near the central valley of Israel, the tremendous volume and flow of blood could easily form troughs four feet deep in some places.

**one thousand six hundred furlongs** (v. 20)—The approximate distance from Armageddon in the north of Palestine to Edom in the south. The great battle will rage across that entire area and even slightly beyond.

**sea of glass** (15:2)—God's heavenly throne sits on a transparent crystal platform or pavement (see 4:6).

**victory over the beast** (v. 2)—All the saints from every nation, including Israel, ultimately triumph over Satan's Antichrist and his system because of their faith in Jesus Christ.

**song of Moses** (v. 3)—Sung by the people of Israel immediately after their passage through the Red Sea and their deliverance from the Egyptian armies, this was a song of victory and deliverance that the redeemed who overcome Antichrist and his system will readily identify with.

song of the Lamb (v. 3)—See 5:8–14. These two songs celebrate two great redemptive events: (1) the deliverance of Israel by God from Egypt through Moses; and (2) the deliverance of sinners by God from sin through Christ.

Great and marvelous are Your works (v. 3)—This statement from the song of the Lamb extols God's powerful works in creation as He providentially upholds the universe (see Ps. 139:14).

Almighty (v. 3)—God is omnipotent.

King of the saints (v. 3)—God is sovereign over the redeemed of every nation.

the temple of the tabernacle of the testimony (v. 5)—This refers to the ark of the covenant in the Holy of Holies (temple) where God dwells (see 11:19).

seven plagues (v. 6)—The final, most severe judgments from God, described in chapter 16 (see v. 1).

linen . . . golden bands (v. 6)—The fabric represents holiness and purity (19:14). These are belts or girdles, running from the shoulder to the waist, that each of the seven angels wears over his garments. The bands demonstrate riches, royalty, and untarnished glory.

filled with smoke (v. 8)—See Exodus 19:16–18; 40:34–35.

the song of the Lamb, saying: "Great and marvelous are Your works, Lord God Almighty! Just and true are Your ways, O King of the saints!

4 Who shall not fear You, O Lord, and glorify Your name? For You alone are holy. For all nations shall come and worship before You, for Your judgments have been manifested."

5 After these things I looked, and behold, the temple of the tabernacle of the testimony in heaven was opened.

6 And out of the temple came the seven angels having the seven plagues, clothed in pure bright linen, and having their chests girded with golden bands.

7 Then one of the four living creatures gave to the seven angels seven golden bowls full of the wrath of God who lives forever and ever.

8 The temple was filled with smoke from the glory of God and from His power, and no one was able to enter the temple till the seven plagues of the seven angels were completed.

16:1 Then I heard a loud voice from the temple saying to the seven angels, "Go and pour out the bowls of the wrath of God on the earth."

2 So the first went and poured out his bowl upon the earth, and a foul and loathsome sore came upon the men who had the mark of the beast and those who worshiped his image.

3 Then the second angel poured out his bowl on the sea, and it became blood as of a dead man; and every living creature in the sea died.

first . . . bowl . . . a foul and loathsome sore (16:2)—The Septuagint (LXX) uses the same Greek word to describe the boils that plagued the Egyptians and afflicted Job (Job 2:7). In the New Testament, it describes the open sores that covered the beggar Lazarus (Luke 16:21). All over the world, people will be afflicted with incurable, open, oozing sores.

mark of the beast (v. 2)—Only the worshipers of Antichrist will be afflicted (see 13:16; see 14:9–11).

second . . . bowl . . . every living creature in the sea died (v. 3)—This is reminiscent of the second trumpet (8:8–9) and of the first plague against Egypt. This plague, however, will be far more widespread. The water in the world's oceans will become thick, dark, and coagulated, like the blood of a corpse. The death and decay of billions of sea creatures will only add to the misery of this judgment.

4  *Then the third angel poured out his bowl on the rivers and springs of water, and they became blood.*

5  *And I heard the angel of the waters saying: "You are righteous, O Lord, The One who is and who was and who is to be, because You have judged these things.*

6  *For they have shed the blood of saints and prophets, and You have given them blood to drink. For it is their just due."*

7  *And I heard another from the altar saying, "Even so, Lord God Almighty, true and righteous are Your judgments."*

8  *Then the fourth angel poured out his bowl on the sun, and power was given to him to scorch men with fire.*

9  *And men were scorched with great heat, and they blasphemed the name of God who has power over these plagues; and they did not repent and give Him glory.*

10  *Then the fifth angel poured out his bowl on the throne of the beast, and his kingdom became full of darkness; and they gnawed their tongues because of the pain.*

**third . . . bowl . . . rivers and springs of water** (v. 4)—Fresh water, already in short supply because of the prolonged drought (11:6), will now suffer the fate of the oceans (see Exod. 7:19–21). In addition to suffering from thirst, the worshipers of Antichrist will have no clean water with which to wash their sores.

**who is and who was and who is to be** (v. 5)—This phrase expresses God's eternality (see 1:4, 8; 4:8; 11:17). Verse 6 says that the eternal God will judge justly because they have killed the believers and preachers of the gospel (6:9–11; 7:9–17; 11:18; 17:6; 18:20). This slaughter will have no parallel in history, and neither will the vengeance of God (see Rom. 12:19–21).

**given them blood to drink** (v. 6)—The thick, blood-like substance which the fresh waters have become is all that is available to drink (see v. 4).

**For it is their just due.** (v. 6)—The angel exonerates God from any charge that His judgments are too harsh. This unspeakably wicked generation will shed more blood than any before it, including that of saints (6:9; 17:6) and prophets (11:7–10). God's judgment is fair and proper (see Exod. 21:25–27; Lev. 24:19–20; Heb. 10:26–31).

**altar** (v. 7)—The personified altar echoes the words of the angel, reinforcing the truth that God is just in all judgment (19:1–2; see Gen. 18:25; Ps. 51:4; Rom. 3:4).

**fourth . . . bowl . . . scorch . . . with fire** (v. 8)—The sun that normally provides light, warmth, and energy will become a deadly killer. With no fresh water to drink, earth's inhabitants will face extreme heat. The scorching heat will melt the polar ice caps, which some estimate would raise the level of the world's oceans by 200 feet, inundating many of the world's major cities and producing further catastrophic loss of life. The resulting disruption of ocean transportation will make it difficult to distribute the dwindling resources of food and water.

**they did not repent** (v. 9)—Incredibly, sinners will still refuse to repent (see vv. 11, 21), and instead blaspheme God—the One they know has caused their afflictions.

**throne of the beast** (v. 10)—This refers to either Antichrist's actual throne, or his capital city, but extends to all his dominion. Regardless of where the darkness begins, it eventually covers Antichrist's entire kingdom.

**full of darkness** (v. 10)—Worldwide darkness is elsewhere associated with the judgment of God.

**gnawed their tongues** (v. 10)—a futile attempt to alleviate the pain from their sores, the drought, and the fierce heat

**blasphemed the God of heaven** (v. 11)—A sign of their continued loyalty to Antichrist and their anger at God for the cumulative miseries brought about by the first five bowls. "God of heaven," a frequent Old Testament title for God, appears in the New Testament only here and in 11:13.

**their sores** (v. 11)—The lingering effects of the first bowl are the chief cause of their blasphemy.

**Euphrates** (v. 12)—Called "the great river" five times in Scripture (see 9:14; Gen. 15:18; Deut. 1:7; Jos. 1:4), it flows some eighteen hundred miles from its source on the slopes of Mt. Ararat to the Persian Gulf (see

11 They blasphemed the God of heaven because of their pains and their sores, and did not repent of their deeds.

12 Then the sixth angel poured out his bowl on the great river Euphrates, and its water was dried up, so that the way of the kings from the east might be prepared.

13 And I saw three unclean spirits like frogs coming out of the mouth of the dragon, out of the mouth of the beast, and out of the mouth of the false prophet.

14 For they are spirits of demons, performing signs, which go out to the kings of the earth and of the whole world, to gather them to the battle of that great day of God Almighty.

15 "Behold, I am coming as a thief. Blessed is he who

9:14). It forms the eastern boundary of the land God promised to Israel (Gen. 15:18; Deut. 1:7; 11:24; Josh. 1:4). With its flow already reduced by the prolonged drought and intensified heat, God will supernaturally dry it up to make way for the eastern confederacy to reach Palestine (Isa. 11:15).

**the kings from the east** (v. 12)—God providentially draws these kings and their armies in order to destroy them in the Battle of Armageddon (v. 14). Their reason for coming may be to rebel against Antichrist, whose failure to alleviate the world's suffering will no doubt erode his popularity. Or, this may be a final act of rabid anti-Semitism intent on destroying Israel, perhaps in retaliation for the plagues sent by her God. Since the sun may have melted the ice caps on Ararat, flooding the valley of the Euphrates as the river overflows its banks and bridges, the land will be swamped. God will have to dry it up miraculously for the eastern army to get to Armageddon.

**three unclean spirits** (v. 13)—A common New Testament designation for demons (see Matt. 12:43; Mark 1:23; Luke 8:29). These are especially vile, powerful, and deceitful (v. 14).

**like frogs** (v. 13)—This figure further emphasizes their vileness (see Lev. 10:11). Frogs were unclean animals according to Old Testament dietary laws (Lev. 11:10–11, 41). Persian mythology viewed them as plague-inducing creatures. The demons are thus described as slimy, cold-blooded, loathsome beings.

**the dragon . . . the beast . . . the false prophet** (v. 13)—The "unholy trinity," composed of Satan (the dragon; see 12:3), the Antichrist (the beast; see 11:7), and Antichrist's associate (the false prophet; see 13:11), spew out this plague.

**signs** (v. 14)—These are supernatural wonders (see 13:12–15) designed to deceive the kings into invading Palestine (see 19:20; 1 Kings 2:20–23; Mark 13:22). Their impact will be so great that the unclean spirits are able to induce the kings to make the journey to Palestine in spite of their sores, the intense heat, drought, and darkness.

**kings of the earth** (v. 14)—No longer just the eastern confederacy, but now all the world begins to gather in Palestine for the final, climactic battle (Ps. 2:2, 3; Joel 3:2–4; Zech. 14:1–3).

**the battle of that great day of God Almighty** (v. 14)—The Battle of Armageddon (v. 16). It is the great war with God and Christ (see 2 Thess. 1:7–10; see Joel 2:11; 3:2, 4). The war will end when Christ arrives (19:17–20).

watches, and keeps his garments, lest he walk naked and they see his shame."

16 And they gathered them together to the place called in Hebrew, Armageddon.

17 Then the seventh angel poured out his bowl into the air, and a loud voice came out of the temple of heaven, from the throne, saying, "It is done!"

18 And there were noises and thunderings and lightnings; and there was a great earthquake, such a mighty and great earthquake as had not occurred since men were on the earth.

19 Now the great city was divided into three parts, and the cities of the nations fell. And great Babylon was remembered before God, to give her the cup of the wine of the fierceness of His wrath.

20 Then every island fled away, and the mountains were not found.

21 And great hail from heaven fell upon men, each hailstone about the weight of a talent. Men blasphemed God because of the plague of the hail, since that plague was exceedingly great.

**watches, and keeps his garments** (v. 15)—Our Lord stresses the need for constant readiness for His return (see 1 John 2:28). The imagery pictures a soldier ready for battle, or a homeowner watchful for the arrival of a thief (see also 3:3; 1 Thess. 5:2, 4; 2 Pet. 3:10).

**Armageddon** (v. 16)—The Hebrew name for Mt. Megiddo, 60 miles north of Jerusalem. The battle will rage on the nearby plains, at the site of Barak's victory over the Canaanites (Judg. 4) and Gideon's victory over the Midianites (Judg. 7). Napoleon called this valley the greatest battlefield he had ever seen. But the Battle of Armageddon will not be limited to the Megiddo plains—it will encompass the length of Palestine (see 14:20).

**seventh . . . bowl . . . "It is done!"** (v. 17)—This bowl will complete God's wrath (except for final judgment on the rebellious at the end of the Millennium; 20:7–10) and immediately precedes the second coming of Christ. It will usher in the worst calamity in the history of the world. The voice from the temple in heaven is undoubtedly that of God Himself. "It is done!" means, "It has been and will remain done" (see John 19:30). God will punctuate the completion of His wrath with a devastating earthquake—the most powerful in earth's history (see 16:19–21).

**the great city** (v. 19)—See 11:13; 21:10; Zechariah 14:1–8. Jerusalem will be split into three parts (Zech. 14:4), not as a judgment (see 11:13), but as an improvement. The additional water supply (Zech. 14:8) and topographical changes (Zech. 14:4–5) will prepare the city for its central place in the millennial kingdom. Jerusalem is the only city to be spared the judgment (see 1 Chron. 23:25; Ps. 125:1–2; Mic. 4:7) and will be made more beautiful (Ps. 48:2) because of her repentance (see 11:13).

**cities of the nations** (v. 19)—God's purpose is very different for the rest of the world's cities—they are to be destroyed.

**Babylon** (v. 19)—The capital of the Antichrist's empire will receive a special outpouring of God's wrath as prophesied in Isaiah 13:6–13. Chapters 17 and 18 give details of its destruction.

**every island fled . . . mountains . . . not found** (v. 20)—This powerful earthquake will radically alter all the earth's topography, preparing it for the coming millennial kingdom. See 6:12–14; Isaiah 40:4–5.

**a talent** (v. 21)—The heaviest weight a normal man could carry (about 75 lbs.). The huge size of the hailstones indicates unparalleled atmospheric convulsions. Such massive chunks of ice will cause unimaginable devastation and death.

1) How are the 144,000 described in chapter 14? What are they doing?

_____

_____

_____

_____

_____

_____

*(Verses to consider: Ps. 40:3; Zeph. 3:13; 2 Cor. 11:2; Eph. 1:4; Col. 1:22)*

2) John saw several different angels in this vision. What were they each doing?

_____

_____

_____

_____

_____

3) What is the "song of Moses" (chapter 15)? What does it say about God?

_____

_____

_____

_____

4) What do you learn about God's great "winepress" of wrath, the great battle (14:19–20; 16:14–19)?

_____

_____

_____

_____

_____

5) The bowl judgments form the content of chapter 16. What is the nature of each of these catastrophes? What was the response of the inhabitants of earth following them?

_____

_____

_____

*(Verses to consider: Exod. 7:20–25; 9:9–11; Isa. 60:2; Jer. 4:23–27; Joel 2:2; Mark 13:24–25)*

6) What glimpses of God's power and triumph do you see throughout these chapters?

_____

_____

_____

_____

## Going Deeper

The redeemed in heaven sang the "song of Moses." Read this song of praise in Exodus 15:1–18.

1 *Then Moses and the children of Israel sang this song to the LORD, and spoke, saying: "I will sing to the LORD, for He has triumphed gloriously! The horse and its rider He has thrown into the sea!*

2 *The LORD is my strength and song, and He has become my salvation; He is my God, and I will praise Him; My father's God, and I will exalt Him.*

3 *The LORD is a man of war; the LORD is His name.*

4 *Pharaoh's chariots and his army He has cast into the sea; His chosen captains also are drowned in the Red Sea.*

5 *The depths have covered them; they sank to the bottom like a stone.*

6 *"Your right hand, O LORD, has become glorious in power; Your right hand, O LORD, has dashed the enemy in pieces.*

7 *And in the greatness of Your excellence You have overthrown those who rose against You; You sent forth Your wrath; It consumed them like stubble.*

8 *And with the blast of Your nostrils the waters were gathered together; the floods stood upright like a heap; the depths congealed in the heart of the sea.*

9 *The enemy said, 'I will pursue, I will overtake, I will divide the spoil; my desire shall be satisfied on them. I will draw my sword, my hand shall destroy them.'*

10 *You blew with Your wind, the sea covered them; they sank like lead in the mighty waters.*

11 *"Who is like You, O Lord, among the gods? Who is like You, glorious in holiness, fearful in praises, doing wonders?*

12 *You stretched out Your right hand; the earth swallowed them.*

13 *You in Your mercy have led forth the people whom You have redeemed; You have guided them in Your strength to Your holy habitation.*

14 *"The people will hear and be afraid; sorrow will take hold of the inhabitants of Philistia.*

15 *Then the chiefs of Edom will be dismayed; the mighty men of Moab, trembling will take hold of them; all the inhabitants of Canaan will melt away.*

16 *Fear and dread will fall on them; by the greatness of Your arm they will be as still as a stone, till Your people pass over, O Lord, till the people pass over whom You have purchased.*

17 *You will bring them in and plant them in the mountain of Your inheritance, in the place, O Lord, which You have made for Your own dwelling, the sanctuary, O Lord, which Your hands have established.*

18 *"The Lord shall reign forever and ever."*

## EXPLORING THE MEANING

7) What things had the Lord done for His people?

_____

_____

_____

_____

_____

8) Identify the themes in this song of Moses that are also found in Revelation 14–16.

_____

_____

_____

_____

_____

9) Read Proverbs 23:17. Why is it important to fear God (see Rev. 14:7)?

_____

_____

_____

*(Verses to consider: Rom. 1:18–21; 1 Pet. 2:17)*

10) Read Philippians 1:6. What does this verse say about perseverance, and how does it support the truth conveyed in Revelation 14:12?

_____

_____

_____

*(Verses to consider: Rom. 8:31–39; Jer. 32:40; Matt. 24:13;*
*John 6:35–40; 10:27–30; 1 John 5:4, 11–13, 20)*

## Truth for Today

The message of the seventh trumpet is that Jesus Christ is the sovereign King of kings and Lord of lords. He will one day take the rule of the earth away from the usurper, Satan, and from earth's petty human rulers. History is moving inexorably toward its culmination in Christ's earthly reign. When He returns, He will bring covenant blessings to the redeemed, but eternal judgment to those who reject Him. In the light of that sobering truth, Peter exclaims, "What manner of persons ought you to be in holy conduct and godliness, looking for and hastening the coming of the day of God?" (2 Pet. 3:11–12).

## Reflecting on the Text

11) Warren Wiersbe has written: "One of the themes that links Revelation 14–16 together is expressed by the word *voice*, which is used eleven times. In the events recorded, God speaks to His people or to the lost world, or His people and angels speak out in praise of the Lord or in warning to the world. As the world moves into the last half of the Tribulation, heaven is not silent." What do you sense the voice of God is saying to *you* in this lesson? Why?

_____

_____

_____

12) Though the Battle of Armageddon is yet future, you are involved in a real spiritual battle in the present (see Eph. 6). How can you be victorious and evade spiritual injury today?

_____

_____

_____

_____

_____

13) List the people in your life who need to embrace the "everlasting gospel" (14:6). What are some practical ways that you can point them to the cross?

_____

_____

_____

_____

_____

## Personal Response

Write out additional reflections, questions you may have, or a prayer.

_____

_____

_____

_____

_____

_____

_____

_____

_____

_____

# 10

## DESTRUCTION AND DEVASTATION!
*Revelation 17:1–18:24*

## DRAWING NEAR

Thinking about the reality of evil helps open our eyes to see the very real spiritual battle we are engaged in every day. What evidences of this spiritual battle have you seen lately in your life?

_____

_____

_____

What resources have been most helpful to you in fighting the good fight?

_____

_____

_____

## THE CONTEXT

Revelation reminds us that there is a cosmic battle going on now and will be going on in the future. No one can be neutral. Each of us is either part of the domain of darkness or part of the kingdom of God. As we yield to one sphere or the other, we become the companions of God or the companions of Satan. To doubt this reality is the gravest mistake any of us can make, because making the wrong choice results in eternal disaster.

God offers all people the life-giving gospel of the Lord Jesus Christ. Satan and the forces of hell lure people to their destruction by dangling before them the "passing pleasures of sin" (Heb. 11:25). There is coming a day when the siren call of hell will be so loud as to be all but irresistible. This passage tells us that people of that time will ignore the repeated powerful preaching of the gospel and the warnings conveyed by the terrifying judgments from God. Having rejected all offers of grace and mercy, they will see death come upon mankind on a scale unprecedented in human history. Yet even then they will not repent; in fact they will curse God. People at that time will have made the irrevocable choice to side with the forces of hell.

This section (chs. 17–18) reveals the dark destiny of this satanic kingdom—called by the symbolic name "Babylon"—and the beast who leads it. We see God's judgment on religious Babylon—the evil "religious" system of the end times, and the destruction of the beast's vast economic and political system.

## KEYS TO THE TEXT

*Babylon:* In the book of Revelation this name refers to the entire worldwide political, economic, and religious kingdom of Antichrist (see Rev. 16:17–19 for details of its fall), not to a real city in John's time. The original city of Babylon was the birthplace of idolatry where the residents built the tower of Babel, a monument to rebelliousness and false religion. Such idolatry was subsequently spread when God confounded humanity's language and scattered them around the world (see Gen. 11:1–9). This passage pictures Babylon causing the world to become intoxicated with her pleasures and enter an orgy of rebellion, hatred, and idolatry toward God. "Fornication" means spiritual prostitution to the Antichrist's false system.

## UNLEASHING THE TEXT

Read 17:1–18:24, noting the key words and definitions next to the passage.

**seven angels** (v. 1)—The reference to these angels links chapters 17 and 18 with the bowl judgments (ch. 16), which extend to the second coming of Christ (see 16:17). Chapters 17 and 18 focus on one aspect of those bowl judgments, the judgment of Babylon. The judgments already described are identified as targeting the final world system.

**Revelation 17:1–18:24 (NKJV)**

1 *Then one of the seven angels who had the seven bowls came and talked with me, saying to me, "Come, I will show you the judgment of the great harlot who sits on many waters,*

2 *with whom the kings of the earth committed fornication, and the inhabitants of the earth were made drunk with the wine of her fornication."*

**great harlot** (v. 1)—See 14:8. Prostitution frequently symbolizes idolatry or religious apostasy. Nineveh (Nah. 3:1, 4), Tyre (Isa. 23:17), and even Jerusalem (Isa. 1:21) are also depicted as harlot cities.

**sits on many waters** (v. 1)—This picture emphasizes the sovereign power of the harlot. The picture is of a ruler seated on a throne, ruling the waters, which symbolize the nations of the world (see v. 15).

**kings . . . committed fornication** (v. 2)—The harlot will ally herself with the world's political leaders. Fornication here does not refer to sexual sin, but to idolatry (see 14:8). All the world rulers will be absorbed into the empire of Satan's false christ.

**wine of her fornication** (v. 2)—The harlot's influence will extend beyond the world's rulers to the rest of mankind (see 15; 13:8, 14). The imagery does not describe actual wine and sexual sin, but pictures the world's people being swept up into the intoxication and sin of a false system of religion.

³ So he carried me away in the Spirit into the wilderness. And I saw a woman sitting on a scarlet beast which was full of names of blasphemy, having seven heads and ten horns.

⁴ The woman was arrayed in purple and scarlet, and adorned with gold and precious stones and pearls, having in her hand a golden cup full of abominations and the filthiness of her fornication.

⁵ And on her forehead a name was written: MYSTERY, BABYLON THE GREAT, THE MOTHER OF HARLOTS AND OF THE ABOMINATIONS OF THE EARTH.

⁶ I saw the woman, drunk with the blood of the saints and with the blood of the martyrs of Jesus. And when I saw her, I marveled with great amazement.

⁷ But the angel said to me, "Why did you marvel? I will tell you the mystery of the woman and of the beast that carries her, which has the seven heads and the ten horns.

**in the Spirit** (v. 3)—See 1:10; 4:2; 21:10. The Holy Spirit transports John into the wilderness (a deserted, lonely, desolate wasteland), perhaps to give him a better understanding of the vision.

**a woman** (v. 3)—the harlot of verse 1, Babylon

**scarlet beast** (v. 3)—This refers to the Antichrist (see 13:1, 4; 14:9; 16:10), who for a time will support and use the false religious system to effect world unity. Then he will assume political control (see v. 16). Scarlet is the color of luxury, splendor, and royalty.

**full of names of blasphemy** (v. 3)—because of his self-deification (see 13:1)

**having seven heads and ten horns** (v. 3)—This pictures the extent of Antichrist's political alliances (see vv. 9–12; 13:1).

**purple and scarlet** (v. 4)—The colors of royalty, nobility, and wealth. The woman is portrayed as a prostitute who has plied her trade successfully and become extremely wealthy.

**adorned** (v. 4)—Prostitutes often dress in fine clothes and precious jewels to allure their victims. The religious harlot Babylon is no different, adorning herself to lure the nations into her grasp.

**a golden cup** (v. 4)—This is yet another evidence of the harlot's great wealth; but the pure gold is defiled by the filthiness of her immorality. Just as a prostitute might first get her victim drunk, so the harlot system deceives the nations into committing spiritual fornication with her.

**forehead** (v. 5)—It was customary for Roman prostitutes to wear a headband with their name on it, parading their wretchedness for all to see. The harlot's forehead is emblazoned with a threefold title descriptive of the world's final false religious system.

**MYSTERY** (v. 5)—A New Testament mystery is truth once hidden, but in the New Testament revealed. Spiritual Babylon's true identity is yet to be revealed. Thus, the precise details of how it will be manifested in the world are not yet known.

**BABYLON THE GREAT** (v. 5)—This Babylon is distinct from the historical, geographical city of Babylon (which still existed in John's day). The details of John's vision cannot be applied to any historical city.

**MOTHER OF HARLOTS** (v. 5)—All false religion stems ultimately from Babel, or Babylon.

**the blood of the saints . . . martyrs of Jesus** (v. 6)—Some see the first group as Old Testament saints and the second as New Testament saints—an unimportant distinction since this pictures the martyrs of the Tribulation. John's point is that the harlot is a murderer. False religion has killed millions of believers over the centuries, and the final false system will be far more deadly than any that preceded it.

**mystery** (v. 7)—not that Babylon is a false system of religion, because that is already known, but that the beast will fully support the harlot, and they will together exert vast influence over the whole earth

105

**The beast** (v. 8)—Both a king and a kingdom are referred to in this term.

**was, and is not, and will ascend** (v. 8)—A reference to the Antichrist's false resurrection (13:3–4, 12–14; see 13:3).

**out of the bottomless pit** (v. 8)—After his "resurrection," the Antichrist will become possessed by a great demon from the abyss (see 13:1, 3).

**perdition** (v. 8)—eternal destruction (see verse 11; Matt. 7:13; John 17:12; Phil. 1:28; 3:19; 2 Pet. 3:7, 16); this is the lake of fire, the place of Antichrist's destruction (19:20)

**Book of Life** (v. 8)—The roll of the elect, written in eternity past by God (see 3:5). Only the elect will escape the Antichrist's deception.

**from the foundation of the world** (v. 8)—see 13:8; this phrase, meaning "before time began," is used frequently (Matt. 13:35; 25:34; Luke 11:50; John 17:24; Eph. 1:4; Heb. 4:3; 9:26; 1 Pet. 1:20) to refer to God's precreation plan.

8 *The beast that you saw was, and is not, and will ascend out of the bottomless pit and go to perdition. And those who dwell on the earth will marvel, whose names are not written in the Book of Life from the foundation of the world, when they see the beast that was, and is not, and yet is.*

9 *"Here is the mind which has wisdom: The seven heads are seven mountains on which the woman sits.*

10 *There are also seven kings. Five have fallen, one is, and the other has not yet come. And when he comes, he must continue a short time.*

11 *The beast that was, and is not, is himself also the eighth, and is of the seven, and is going to perdition.*

12 *"The ten horns which you saw are ten kings who have received no kingdom as yet, but they receive authority for one hour as kings with the beast.*

13 *These are of one mind, and they will give their power and authority to the beast.*

**seven mountains** (v. 9)—The Greek word is often used of hills (Matt. 5:1; 15:29; John 6:15; 8:1). Many commentators interpret this expression to mean Rome, which sits on seven hills. It is true that the final worldwide system of false religion includes, but is not necessarily limited to, Rome; but specifically, the seven mountains in context likely symbolize the seven kingdoms and their kings of verse 10.

**seven kings** (v. 10)—representatives of the seven great world empires (Egypt, Assyria, Babylon, Medo-Persia, Greece, Rome, and that of the Antichrist)

**Five have fallen, one is, and the other** (v. 10)—When John wrote this book, the Egyptian, Assyrian, Babylonian, Medo-Persian and Greek empires had gone out of existence; Rome still existed; and the Antichrist's empire had not yet come. When it does, it will be brief (12:12; 13:5) and will end in perdition (v. 11; see also v. 8).

**and is not . . . the eighth** (v. 11)—The Antichrist's kingdom is said to be both the seventh and eighth kingdoms because of his supposed demise and resurrection. He is the seventh king before and the eighth king after his "resurrection," when he destroys the harlot's religious empire and demands exclusive worship of himself (v. 16).

**ten kings** (v. 12)—See 12:3; 13:1. These kings are sub-rulers under the Antichrist, whose empire will apparently be divided into ten administrative districts.

**no kingdom as yet** (v. 12)—Thus, the kings cannot be identified with any historical figures.

**one hour** (v. 12)—symbolic of the brief three-and-one-half-year-period of time (see 11:2–3; 12:6, 12, 14; 13:5; 18:10, 17, 19).

14 *These will make war with the Lamb, and the Lamb will overcome them, for He is Lord of lords and King of kings; and those who are with Him are called, chosen, and faithful."*

15 *Then he said to me, "The waters which you saw, where the harlot sits, are peoples, multitudes, nations, and tongues.*

16 *And the ten horns which you saw on the beast, these will hate the harlot, make her desolate and naked, eat her flesh and burn her with fire.*

17 *For God has put it into their hearts to fulfill His purpose, to be of one mind, and to give their kingdom to the beast, until the words of God are fulfilled.*

18 *And the woman whom you saw is that great city which reigns over the kings of the earth."*

18:1 *After these things I saw another angel coming down from heaven, having great authority, and the earth was illuminated with his glory.*

2 *And he cried mightily with a loud voice, saying, "Babylon the great is fallen, is fallen, and has become a dwelling place of demons, a prison for every foul spirit, and a cage for every unclean and hated bird!*

3 *For all the nations have drunk of the wine of the wrath of her fornication, the kings of the earth have committed fornication with her, and the merchants of the earth have become rich through the abundance of her luxury."*

**make war** (v. 14)—a reference to the Battle of Armageddon (16:14–16), where the Lamb will utterly destroy the kings (19:17–21)

**Lord of lords and King of kings** (v. 14)—a title for God (19:16) that emphasizes His sovereignty over all other rulers to whom He has delegated authority

**these will hate the harlot** (v. 16)—After using the false religious system to unify the world kingdoms and gain control of all, the Antichrist—with the help of his ten sub-rulers—will turn against the system, plunder and destroy it, and seize all power and worship for himself. They will be carrying out God's will (v. 17).

**great city** (v. 18)—Here is another identification of the capital city of Babylon, centerpiece of Antichrist's empire (see 18:10, 18, 21).

**earth was illuminated with his glory** (18:1)—The fifth bowl (16:10) will have plunged the world into darkness. Against that backdrop, the sudden, blazing appearance of another angel (not the same as in 17:1, 7, 15) will certainly rivet the world's attention on him and his message of judgment on Babylon (see 14:8).

**Babylon the great is fallen** (v. 2)—See 14:8. The Greek text views the results of this as if it had already taken place (see 14:8). But the seventh bowl is being referred to here, and it is yet to come at this point (16:17–21). When it comes, devastation and annihilation will take place, leaving the place to demons and scavenger birds.

**wine . . . of her fornication** (v. 3)—Religious Babylon (ch. 17) lures the nations into spiritual drunkenness and fornication with false gods (17:2, 4); commercial Babylon (ch. 18) seduces the unbelieving world into a materialistic stupor, so that the people of the world will become drunk with passion because of their relationship with Babylon.

**kings . . . merchants** (v. 3)—Political rulers and corporate leaders alike are swept up in this worldwide system of commerce (14:8; 17:2).

**Come out of her, my people** (v. 4)—God will call His own to disentangle themselves from this evil system. This may also be God's calling the elect to abandon the world system and come to faith in the Savior. In either case, the message is to abandon the system before it is destroyed. The judgment of God on that society living in sinful, arrogant self-indulgence can be avoided.

**remembered** (v. 5)—See 16:19. God does not remember the iniquities of His people (Jer. 31:34), but does remember to protect them (Mal. 3:16–4:2). For unrepentant Babylon, there will be no such forgiveness, only judgment.

**repay** (vv. 6–7)—The angel calls for God to recompense wrath to Babylon in her own cup to repay her according to her deeds (see 17:4). This is an echo of the Old Testament law of retaliation (Exod. 21:24), which will be implemented by God (Rom. 12:17–21).

**double** (v. 6)—has the sense of "full" or "overflowing"; the punishment will fit the crime (see Jer. 16:18)

**cup** (v. 6)—The cup of wickedness from which so many have drunk (14:8; 17:2, 4, 6) will call for the cup of wrath (14:10; 16:19).

4 *And I heard another voice from heaven saying, "Come out of her, my people, lest you share in her sins, and lest you receive of her plagues.*

5 *For her sins have reached to heaven, and God has remembered her iniquities.*

6 *Render to her just as she rendered to you, and repay her double according to her works; in the cup which she has mixed, mix double for her.*

7 *In the measure that she glorified herself and lived luxuriously, in the same measure give her torment and sorrow; for she says in her heart, 'I sit as queen, and am no widow, and will not see sorrow.'*

8 *Therefore her plagues will come in one day—death and mourning and famine. And she will be utterly burned with fire, for strong is the Lord God who judges her.*

9 *"The kings of the earth who committed fornication and lived luxuriously with her will weep and lament for her, when they see the smoke of her burning,*

10 *standing at a distance for fear of her torment, saying, 'Alas, alas, that great city Babylon, that mighty city! For in one hour your judgment has come.'*

11 *"And the merchants of the earth will weep and mourn over her, for no one buys their merchandise anymore:*

12 *merchandise of gold and silver, precious stones and pearls, fine linen and purple, silk and scarlet, every*

**am no widow** (v. 7)—a proud, but empty, boast of self-sufficiency, also made by historical Babylon

**her plagues** (v. 8)—These could include those of 16:1–21, but must be the special destruction of the city as well, described as "death, mourning and famine."

**in one day** (v. 8)—See verses 10, 17. The special judgments on Babylon take place in a brief period of time.

**kings** (v. 9)—The political leaders of the world will weep because the loss of this capital city will signal the doom of Antichrist's empire, and with it, the source of their power. See verse 3; 17:2.

**weep and lament for her** (v. 9)—"Weep" means "to sob openly." "Lament" translates the same Greek word used to express the despair of the unbelieving world at the return of Christ (1:7).

**purple** (v. 12)—This refers to garments laboriously dyed with purple dye extracted from shellfish. Lydia (Acts 16:14) was a seller of such expensive garments. A distinctive mark of the Caesars was their purple robes.

kind of citron wood, every kind of object of ivory, every kind of object of most precious wood, bronze, iron, and marble;

13 and cinnamon and incense, fragrant oil and frankincense, wine and oil, fine flour and wheat, cattle and sheep, horses and chariots, and bodies and souls of men.

14 The fruit that your soul longed for has gone from you, and all the things which are rich and splendid have gone from you, and you shall find them no more at all.

15 The merchants of these things, who became rich by her, will stand at a distance for fear of her torment, weeping and wailing,

16 and saying, 'Alas, alas, that great city that was clothed in fine linen, purple, and scarlet, and adorned with gold and precious stones and pearls!

17 For in one hour such great riches came to nothing.' Every shipmaster, all who travel by ship, sailors, and as many as trade on the sea, stood at a distance

18 and cried out when they saw the smoke of her burning, saying, 'What is like this great city?'

19 "They threw dust on their heads and cried out, weeping and wailing, and saying, 'Alas, alas, that great city, in which all who had ships on the sea became rich by her wealth! For in one hour she is made desolate.'

20 "Rejoice over her, O heaven, and you holy apostles and prophets, for God has avenged you on her!"

21 Then a mighty angel took up a stone like a great millstone and threw it into the sea, saying, "Thus with violence the great city Babylon shall be thrown down, and shall not be found anymore.

*citron wood* (v. 12)—Wood from North African citrus trees, highly valued because of its color, was used to make extremely expensive pieces of furniture.

*marble* (v. 12)—Marble, imported from Africa, Egypt, and Greece, was widely used in Roman buildings.

*fragrant oil* (v. 13)—a very costly perfume (see Matt. 26:7, 12; John 12:3)

*frankincense* (v. 13)—a fragrant gum or resin imported from Arabia and used in incense and perfume (Song of Sol. 3:6; Matt. 2:11)

*bodies and souls of men* (v. 13)—The slave trade, long banned by the civilized nations of the world, will reappear in Antichrist's debauched commercial system.

*shipmaster* (v. 17)—Ship captains will mourn the loss of Babylon and the lucrative transport business that went with it.

*threw dust on their heads* (v. 19)—an ancient expression of grief (see Josh. 7:6; 1 Sam. 4:12; 2 Sam. 1:2; 15:32; Job 2:12)

*in one hour* (v. 19)—not just sixty minutes, but one brief period of swift judgment (see v. 8)

**God has avenged you on her** (v. 20)—The angel will exhort the tribulation martyrs (6:9–11) to rejoice, not over the deaths of those doomed to eternal hell, but because God's righteousness and justice will have prevailed.

*great millstone* (v. 21)—Millstones were large, heavy stones used to grind grain. This metaphor portrays the violence of Babylon's overthrow.

**shall not be heard** (vv. 22–23)—
The fall of Babylon ends whatever semblance of normalcy will still exist in the world after all the seals, trumpets, and bowls. Life will be totally disrupted and the end near. No more music, no industry, no preparing of food ("millstone"), no more power for light, and no more weddings, because God will destroy the deceivers and deceived.

**blood of prophets and saints** (v. 24)—The religious and commercial/political systems embodied in Babylon will commit unspeakable atrocities against

22 The sound of harpists, musicians, flutists, and
   trumpeters shall not be heard in you anymore.
   No craftsman of any craft shall be found in you
   anymore, and the sound of a millstone shall not be
   heard in you anymore.
23 The light of a lamp shall not shine in you anymore,
   and the voice of bridegroom and bride shall not be
   heard in you anymore. For your merchants were the
   great men of the earth, for by your sorcery all the
   nations were deceived.
24 And in her was found the blood of prophets and
   saints, and of all who were slain on the earth."

God's people (see 6:10; 11:7; 13:7, 15; 17:6; 19:2). God will avenge that slaughter of His people (19:2).

1) The scene in chapter 17 opens with the image of a harlot. What does it mean to commit spiritual adultery?

_____

_____

_____

(Verses to consider: Jer. 3:6–9; Ezek. 16:30; 20:30; Hos. 4:15; 5:3; 6:10; 9:1)

2) What title did John see written on the harlot's forehead and what does it mean?

_____

_____

_____

3) List all the images of final destruction that you find in these chapters.

_____

_____

_____

4) How do the kings and merchants respond upon hearing the news of Babylon's destruction in chapter 18? In what did they have their security?

_____

_____

_____

_____

5) What is God's message to His own people in chapter 18?

_____

_____

_____

_____

_____

*(Verses to consider: Isa. 48:20; Jer. 50:8; 51:6–9, 45; 2 Cor. 6:17; 1 John 2:15)*

## GOING DEEPER

The book of Daniel records several visions of the end times. The king of Babylon, King Nebuchadnezzar, asked Daniel to interpret a dream he had about an image of gold with feet of clay that was broken in pieces by a stone. Read Daniel 2:36–45.

36 *This is the dream. Now we will tell the interpretation of it before the king.*
37 *You, O king, are a king of kings. For the God of heaven has given you a kingdom, power, strength, and glory;*
38 *and wherever the children of men dwell, or the beasts of the field and the birds of the heaven, He has given them into your hand, and has made you ruler over them all—you are this head of gold.*
39 *But after you shall arise another kingdom inferior to yours; then another, a third kingdom of bronze, which shall rule over all the earth.*
40 *And the fourth kingdom shall be as strong as iron, inasmuch as iron breaks in pieces and shatters everything; and like iron that crushes, that kingdom will break in pieces and crush all the others.*
41 *Whereas you saw the feet and toes, partly of potter's clay and partly of iron, the kingdom shall be divided; yet the strength of the iron shall be in it, just as you saw the iron mixed with ceramic clay.*
42 *And as the toes of the feet were partly of iron and partly of clay, so the kingdom shall be partly strong and partly fragile.*

43 *As you saw iron mixed with ceramic clay, they will mingle with the seed of men; but they will not adhere to one another, just as iron does not mix with clay.*

44 *And in the days of these kings the God of heaven will set up a kingdom which shall never be destroyed; and the kingdom shall not be left to other people; it shall break in pieces and consume all these kingdoms, and it shall stand forever.*

45 *Inasmuch as you saw that the stone was cut out of the mountain without hands, and that it broke in pieces the iron, the bronze, the clay, the silver, and the gold—the great God has made known to the king what will come to pass after this. The dream is certain, and its interpretation is sure."*

## EXPLORING THE MEANING

6) What will happen to Nebuchadnezzar's powerful Babylonian kingdom?

_____

_____

_____

_____

_____

*(Verses to consider: Dan. 5:30–31)*

7) What insight does Daniel's vision give into the meaning of the beast and the seven kings in Revelation 17:3, 8–16?

_____

_____

_____

_____

8) How does Daniel describe God's ultimate kingdom (v. 44)?

_____

_____

_____

_____

## TRUTH FOR TODAY

Despite all the terrifying judgments, which by this time all people will acknowledge to be from God, and the worldwide preaching of the gospel (Matt. 24:14) by the 144,000 and others, people will still refuse to believe. It seems incredible that, having experienced the fury of God's judgment and having heard the message of salvation, people will stubbornly cling to their sin. But the sad truth is that "the light has come into the world, and men loved darkness rather than light, because their deeds were evil. For everyone practicing evil hates the light and does not come to the light, lest his deeds should be exposed" (John 3:19–20).

The unbelieving world rejected Jesus when He came, it rejects the life-giving message of the gospel now, and it will continue to reject the truth during the future outpouring of God's wrath and judgment. Having gone on sinning willfully after receiving the knowledge of the truth, wicked people have nothing to look forward to except a terrifying expectation of judgment (Heb. 10:26–27).

## REFLECTING ON THE TEXT

9) What gives you hope, knowing that so great a judgment of God will come in the future?

_____

_____

_____

_____

_____

10) The merchants and businessmen served money as their god, and they lost everything in these heavenly scenes of destruction. How can you be a wise steward of the money with which God has entrusted you, without becoming caught up in the "materialistic Babylonian spirit" that permeates contemporary culture?

_____

_____

_____

_____

_____

11) If the current world system is doomed and destined for destruction, what practical steps can you take to make sure you and your family can live "in the world" and not become ensnared by its values?

_____

_____

_____

_____

_____

## Personal Response

Write out additional reflections, questions you may have, or a prayer.

_____

_____

_____

_____

_____

_____

_____

_____

_____

_____

_____

_____

_____

_____

# 11

# CHRIST AND HIS KINGDOM

*Revelation 19:1–20:15*

## DRAWING NEAR

John's vision of the last days turns a corner here, when the King of kings returns to rule and reign in righteousness! What are you most looking forward to about Jesus' second coming?

---

The Bible makes it clear that we will be judged and rewarded according to our works. How does knowing Jesus will come again affect how you live each day?

---

## THE CONTEXT

How will the world end? There are as many answers to that question as there are doomsday prophets, futurists, and scientists. Some speculate about collisions with giant asteroids. Others worry about nuclear conflagration. Still others fret over possible extraterrestrial invasion or the extinction of the human race due to pollution or disease. But those who study the Bible know that "history" is, literally, "His story." God is, and always has been, sovereign over the events of earth. The New Testament book of Revelation repeatedly reminds us of this truth. The day is coming when the Lord Jesus Christ will return to reward His followers and to punish His enemies.

Few passages in all of Scripture are as majestic and powerful as Revelation 19–20! It begins with the sound of rejoicing over the defeat of the evil world system called Babylon. It ends with the Battle of Armageddon and Christ's glorious second coming—events that mark the close of the Tribulation. Then we see the binding of Satan, Christ's thousand-year earthly kingdom, Satan's final rebellion, and the Great White Throne Judgment. In the end, Jesus Christ will make all things right. Alleluia!

## KEYS TO THE TEXT

*The Millennium:* This is the thousand-year reign of Christ over the earth (20:2–7). There are three main views regarding the duration and nature of this period:

(1) *Premillennialism* says Christ will return before the thousand-year reign and sees this as a *literal* thousand-year period during which Jesus Christ reigns on the earth, in fulfillment of numerous Old Testament prophecies (for example, Ps. 2; Isa. 11:6–12; 24:23; Hos. 3:4–5; Joel 3:9–21; Amos 9:8–15; and Zech. 14:1–11). Premillennialism says that Christ will return after the events of the Great Tribulation but before the final judgments and the establishment of the new heavens and new earth. Using the same general principles of interpretation for both prophetic and non-prophetic passages leads most naturally to premillennialism. Another strong argument supporting this view is that many biblical prophecies have already been literally fulfilled, suggesting that future prophecies will likewise be fulfilled literally.

(2) *Postmillennialism* says Christ will return after the thousand years and understands the reference to a thousand-year period as only *symbolic* of a golden age of righteousness and spiritual prosperity. It will be ushered in by the spread of the gospel during the present church age and brought to completion when Christ returns. According to this view, references to Christ's reign on earth primarily describe His spiritual reign in the hearts of believers in the church. Postmillennialism essentially teaches that the church, by preaching the gospel, will "Christianize" the world and usher in a worldwide era of peace commonly called the "millennium." Following this Golden Age, Christ will return and eternity will begin.

(3) *Amillennialism* understands the thousand years to be merely symbolic of a long period of time. This view interprets Old Testament prophecies of a millennium as being fulfilled spiritually now in the church (either on earth or in heaven) or as references to the eternal state. But, using the literal, historical, grammatical principles of interpretation so as to determine the normal sense of language, one is left with the inescapable conclusion that Christ will return and reign in a real kingdom on earth for a thousand years. There is nothing in the text to render the conclusion that "a thousand years" is symbolic. Never in Scripture when "year" is used with a number is its meaning not literal.

## UNLEASHING THE TEXT

Read 19:1–20:15, noting the key words and definitions next to the passage.

# Revelation 19:1–20:15 (NKJV)

1 *After these things I heard a loud voice of a great multitude in heaven, saying, "Alleluia! Salvation and glory and honor and power belong to the Lord our God!*

2 *For true and righteous are His judgments, because He has judged the great harlot who corrupted the earth with her fornication; and He has avenged on her the blood of His servants shed by her."*

3 *Again they said, "Alleluia! Her smoke rises up forever and ever!"*

4 *And the twenty-four elders and the four living creatures fell down and worshiped God who sat on the throne, saying, "Amen! Alleluia!"*

5 *Then a voice came from the throne, saying, "Praise our God, all you His servants and those who fear Him, both small and great!"*

6 *And I heard, as it were, the voice of a great multitude, as the sound of many waters and as the sound of mighty thunderings, saying, "Alleluia! For the Lord God Omnipotent reigns!*

7 *Let us be glad and rejoice and give Him glory, for the marriage of the Lamb has come, and His wife has made herself ready."*

**After these things** (v. 1)—This is a time key, meaning after the destruction of Babylon at the end of the Great Tribulation, and just before the kingdom is established (ch. 20). This section bridges the Tribulation and the millennial kingdom.

**great multitude** (v. 1)—probably angels, since the saints join in later (vv. 6–7; see 5:11–12; 7:11–12); the imminent return of the Lord Jesus Christ prompts this outburst of praise

**Alleluia** (v. 1)—The transliteration of this Hebrew word appears four times in the New Testament, all in this chapter (vv. 1, 3, 4, 6). This exclamation, meaning "Praise the Lord," occurs frequently in the Old Testament (see Ps. 105:45; 106:1; 111:1; 112:1; 113:1; 117:1). Five reasons for their praise emerge: (1) God's deliverance of His people from their enemies (v. 1); (2) God's meting out of justice (v. 2); (3) God's permanent crushing of human rebellion (v. 3); (4) God's sovereignty (v. 6); and (5) God's communion with His people (v. 7).

**judgments** (v. 2)—Saints long for the day of judgment (see 6:10). Godly people love righteousness and hate sin, for righteousness honors God and sin mocks Him. Believers long for a world of justice, and it will come (v. 15; 2:27; 12:5).

**smoke rises** (v. 3)—This is because of the fire (see 14:8–11; 17:16, 18; 18:8–9, 18).

**twenty-four elders** (v. 4)—best understood as representatives of the church (see 4:4)

**four living creatures** (v. 4)—a special order of angelic beings (see 4:6). These compose the same group as in 7:11 and are frequently associated with worship (4:8, 11; 5:9–12, 14; 11:16–18)

**small and great** (v. 5)—All distinctions and ranks are to be transcended.

**Omnipotent** (v. 6)—or "Almighty"; used nine times in Revelation as a title for God (see v. 15; 1:8; 4:8; 11:17; 15:3; 16:7, 14; 21:22); the great praise of the multitude sounds like a massive crashing of waves

**marriage of the Lamb** (v. 7)—Hebrew weddings consisted of three phases: (1) betrothal (often when the couple were children); (2) presentation (the festivities, often lasting several days, that preceded the ceremony); and (3) the ceremony (the exchanging of vows). The church was betrothed to Christ by His sovereign choice in eternity past and will be presented to Him at the Rapture. The final supper will signify the end of the ceremony. This symbolic meal will take place at the establishment of the millennial kingdom and last throughout that thousand-year period (see 21:2). While the term "bride" often refers to the church, as it does here, it ultimately expands to include all the redeemed of all ages, which becomes clear in the remainder of the book.

**righteous acts of the saints** (v. 8)—not Christ's imputed righteousness granted to believers at salvation, but the practical results of that righteousness in believers' lives, that is, the outward manifestation of inward virtue

**those who are called** (v. 9)—This is not the bride (the church) but the guests. The bride doesn't get invited, she invites. These are those saved before Pentecost, all the faithful believers saved by grace through faith up to the birth of the church (Acts 2). Though they are not the bride, they still are glorified and reign with Christ in the millennial kingdom. It is really differing imagery rather than differing reality. The guests will also include tribulation saints and

8 And to her it was granted to be arrayed in fine linen, clean and bright, for the fine linen is the righteous acts of the saints.

9 Then he said to me, "Write: 'Blessed are those who are called to the marriage supper of the Lamb!' " And he said to me, "These are the true sayings of God."

10 And I fell at his feet to worship him. But he said to me, "See that you do not do that! I am your fellow servant, and of your brethren who have the testimony of Jesus. Worship God! For the testimony of Jesus is the spirit of prophecy."

11 Now I saw heaven opened, and behold, a white horse. And He who sat on him was called Faithful and True, and in righteousness He judges and makes war.

believers alive in earthly bodies in the kingdom. The church is the bride, pure and faithful—never a harlot, like Israel was (see Hos. 2). So the church is the bride during the presentation feast in heaven, then comes to earth for the celebration of the final meal (the Millennium). After that event, the new order comes and the marriage is consummated (see 21:1–2).

**true sayings of God** (v. 9)—This refers to everything since 17:1. It is all true—the marriage will take place after judgment.

**fell at his feet** (v. 10)—Overwhelmed by the grandeur of the vision, John collapsed in worship before the angel (see 1:17; 22:8).

**do not do that** (v. 10)—See 22:8–9. The Bible forbids the worship of angels.

**the testimony of Jesus is the spirit of prophecy** (v. 10)—The central theme of both Old Testament prophecy and New Testament preaching is the gospel of the Lord Jesus Christ.

**heaven opened** (v. 11)—The One who ascended to heaven and had been seated at the Father's right hand (Heb. 8:1; 10:12) will return to take back the earth from the usurper and establish His kingdom (5:1–10). The nature of this event shows how it differs from the Rapture. At the Rapture, Christ meets His own in the air; in this event He comes with them to earth. At the Rapture, there is no judgment; in this event it is all judgment. This event is preceded by blackness—the darkened sun, moon gone out, stars fallen, smoke—then lightning and blinding glory as Jesus comes. Such details are not included in Rapture passages (John 14:1–3; 1 Thess. 4:13–18).

**white horse** (v. 11)—In the Roman triumphal processions, the victorious general rode his white war horse up the Via Sacra to the temple of Jupiter on the Capitoline Hill. Jesus' first coming was in humiliation on a colt (Zech. 9:9). John's vision portrays Him as the conqueror on His war horse, coming to destroy the wicked, to overthrow the Antichrist, to defeat Satan, and to take control of the earth.

**Faithful and True** (v. 11)—True to His word, Jesus will return to earth (see 3:14).

**in righteousness He judges** (v. 11)—See 20:11–15.

**makes war** (v. 11)—This startling statement, appearing only here and 2:16, vividly portrays the holy wrath of God against sinners. God's patience with sinful, rebellious mankind will be exhausted.

12 *His eyes were like a flame of fire, and on His head were many crowns. He had a name written that no one knew except Himself.*

13 *He was clothed with a robe dipped in blood, and His name is called The Word of God.*

14 *And the armies in heaven, clothed in fine linen, white and clean, followed Him on white horses.*

15 *Now out of His mouth goes a sharp sword, that with it He should strike the nations. And He Himself will rule them with a rod of iron. He Himself treads the winepress of the fierceness and wrath of Almighty God.*

16 *And He has on His robe and on His thigh a name written: KING OF KINGS AND LORD OF LORDS.*

17 *Then I saw an angel standing in the sun; and he cried with a loud voice, saying to all the birds that fly in the midst of heaven, "Come and gather together for the supper of the great God,*

18 *that you may eat the flesh of kings, the flesh of captains, the flesh of mighty men, the flesh of horses and of those who sit on them, and the flesh of all people, free and slave, both small and great."*

19 *And I saw the beast, the kings of the earth, and their armies, gathered together to make war against Him who sat on the horse and against His army.*

**His eyes were like a flame of fire** (v. 12)—Nothing escapes His penetrating vision, so His judgments are always just and accurate (see 1:14; 2:18).

**a name . . . no one knew** (v. 12)—John could see the name, but was unable to comprehend it (see 2 Cor. 12:4). There are unfathomable mysteries in the Godhead that even glorified saints will be unable to grasp.

**a robe dipped in blood** (v. 13)—This is not from the Battle of Armageddon, which will not have begun until verse 15. Christ's blood-spattered garments symbolize the great battles He has already fought against sin, Satan, and death.

**The Word** (v. 13)—Only John uses this title for the Lord. As the Word of God, Jesus is the image of the invisible God; the express image of His person; and the final, full revelation from God.

**armies in heaven** (v. 14)—Composed of the church (v. 8), tribulation saints (7:13), Old Testament believers, and even angels. They return not to help Jesus in the battle (they are unarmed), but to reign with Him after He defeats His enemies (20:4).

**sharp sword** (v. 15)—This symbolizes Christ's power to kill His enemies (1:16). That the sword comes out of His mouth indicates that He wins the battle with the power of His word. Though the saints return with Christ to reign and rule, they are not the executioners. That is His task, and that of His angels.

**rod of iron** (v. 15)—Swift, righteous judgment will mark Christ's rule in the kingdom. Believers will share His authority (see 2:2, 27; 12:5).

**winepress** (v. 15)—a vivid symbol of judgment (see 14:19)

**on His thigh** (v. 16)—Jesus will wear a banner across His robe and down His thigh with a title emblazoned on it that emphasizes His absolute sovereignty over all human rulers (see 17:14).

**supper of the great God** (v. 17)—Also called "the battle of that great day of God Almighty" (16:14), it will begin with an angel summoning birds to feed on the corpses of those who will be slain (see Matt. 24:27–28). God will declare His victory before the battle even begins. The Old Testament frequently pictures the indignity of carrion birds feasting on human dead (Ps. 79:2; Isa. 18:6; Jer. 16:4; 19:7; 34:20; Ezek. 29:5).

**His army** (v. 19)—Zechariah describes this army of the Lord as "all the saints" (14:5).

**beast was captured, and . . . the false prophet** (v. 20)—In an instant, the world's armies are without their leaders. The beast is Antichrist (see 13:1–4); the false prophet is his religious cohort (see 13:11–17).

**cast alive** (v. 20)—The bodies of the beast and the false prophet will be transformed, and they will be banished directly to the lake of fire—the first of countless millions of unregenerate men (20:15) and fallen angels (see Matt. 25:41) to arrive in that dreadful place. That these two still appear there a thousand years later (20:10) refutes the false doctrine of annihilationism (see 14:11; Isa. 66:24; Matt. 25:41; Mark 9:48; Luke 3:17; 2 Thess. 1:9).

**lake of fire** (v. 20)—the final hell, the place of eternal punishment for all unrepentant rebels, angelic or human (see 20:10, 15)

20 *Then the beast was captured, and with him the false prophet who worked signs in his presence, by which he deceived those who received the mark of the beast and those who worshiped his image. These two were cast alive into the lake of fire burning with brimstone.*

21 *And the rest were killed with the sword which proceeded from the mouth of Him who sat on the horse. And all the birds were filled with their flesh.*

20:1 *Then I saw an angel coming down from heaven, having the key to the bottomless pit and a great chain in his hand.*

2 *He laid hold of the dragon, that serpent of old, who is the Devil and Satan, and bound him for a thousand years;*

3 *and he cast him into the bottomless pit, and shut him up, and set a seal on him, so that he should deceive the nations no more till the thousand years were finished. But after these things he must be released for a little while.*

**fire . . . brimstone** (v. 20)—See 9:17. These two are frequently associated with divine judgment (14:10; 20:10; 21:8).

**birds were filled with their flesh** (v. 21)—All remaining sinners in the world will have been executed, and the birds will gorge themselves on their corpses.

**bottomless pit** (20:1)—the place where demons are incarcerated pending their final sentencing to the lake of fire (see 9:1)

**laid hold** (v. 2)—This includes not only Satan but also the demons. Their imprisonment will dramatically alter the world during the kingdom, since their destructive influence in all areas of human thought and life will be removed.

**dragon** (v. 2)—Likening Satan to a dragon emphasizes his ferocity and cruelty (see 12:3).

**serpent of old** (v. 2)—a reference to Satan's first appearance in the Garden of Eden (Gen. 3:1–6), where he deceived Eve (see 2 Cor. 11:3; 1 Tim. 2:14)

**a thousand years** (v. 2)—This is the first of six references to the length of the millennial kingdom (see vv. 3–7).

**bottomless pit** (v. 3)—All seven times that this appears in Revelation, it refers to the place where fallen angels and evil spirits are kept captive, waiting to be sent to the lake of fire—the final hell prepared for them.

**released for a little while** (v. 3)—Satan will be released so God can make a permanent end of sin before establishing the new heaven and earth. All who survive the Tribulation and enter the kingdom will be believers. However, despite that and the personal presence and rule of the Lord Jesus Christ, many of their descendants will refuse to believe in Him. Satan will then gather those unbelievers for one final, futile rebellion against God. It will be quickly and decisively crushed, followed by the Great White Throne judgment and the establishment of the eternal state.

**4** And I saw thrones, and they sat on them, and judgment was committed to them. Then I saw the souls of those who had been beheaded for their witness to Jesus and for the word of God, who had not worshiped the beast or his image, and had not received his mark on their foreheads or on their hands. And they lived and reigned with Christ for a thousand years.

**5** But the rest of the dead did not live again until the thousand years were finished. This is the first resurrection.

**6** Blessed and holy is he who has part in the first resurrection. Over such the second death has no power, but they shall be priests of God and of Christ, and shall reign with Him a thousand years.

**7** Now when the thousand years have expired, Satan will be released from his prison

**8** and will go out to deceive the nations which are in the four corners of the earth, Gog and Magog, to gather them together to battle, whose number is as the sand of the sea.

**the souls of those who had been beheaded** (v. 4)—These are tribulation martyrs (see 6:9; 18:24; 19:2). The Greek word translated "beheaded" became a general term for execution, not necessarily a particular method.

**his mark** (v. 4)—See 13:16. Tribulation martyrs will be executed for refusing the mark of the beast.

**reigned** (v. 4)—Tribulation believers, along with the redeemed from both the Old Testament and New Testament eras, will reign with Christ (1 Cor. 6:2; 2 Tim. 2:12) during the thousand year kingdom.

**the rest of the dead** (v. 5)—The bodies of unbelievers of all ages will not be resurrected until the Great White Throne judgment (vv. 12–13).

**first resurrection** (v. 5)—Scripture teaches two kinds of resurrections: the "resurrection of life" and "the resurrection of condemnation" (John 5:29; see Dan. 12:2; Acts 24:15). The first kind of resurrection is described as "the resurrection of the just" (Luke 14:14), the resurrection of "those who are Christ's at His coming" (1 Cor. 15:23), and the "better resurrection" (Heb. 11:35). It includes only the redeemed of the church age (1 Thess. 4:13–18), the Old Testament (Dan. 12:2), and the Tribulation (v. 4). They will enter the kingdom in resurrection bodies, along with believers who survived the Tribulation. The second kind of resurrection, then, will be the resurrection of the unconverted, who will receive their final bodies suited for torment in hell.

**Blessed** (v. 6)—Those who die in the Lord (14:13) are blessed with the privilege of entering His kingdom (see 1:3).

**second death** (v. 6)—The first death is spiritual and physical, the second is eternal in the lake of fire, the final, eternal hell (v. 14). It could exist outside the created universe as we know it, outside of space and time, and be presently unoccupied (see 19:20).

**Satan . . . released** (v. 7)—He is loosed to bring cohesive leadership to the world of rebels born to the believers who entered the kingdom at the beginning. He is loosed to reveal the character of Christ—rejecting sinners who are brought into judgment for the last time ever.

**Gog and Magog** (v. 8)—The name given to the army of rebels and its leader at the end of the Millennium. They were names of ancient enemies of the Lord. Magog was the grandson of Noah (Gen. 10:2) and founder of a kingdom located north of the Black and Caspian Seas. Gog is apparently the leader of a rebel army known collectively as Magog. The battle depicted in verses 8 and 9 is like the one in Ezekiel 38, 39; it is best to see this one as taking place at the end of the Millennium.

**beloved city** (v. 9)—Jerusalem (see Ps. 78:68), the capital city during Christ's millennial reign. The saints will be living around the city where Christ reigns (see Isa. 24:23).

**fire** (v. 9)—Frequently associated in Scripture with divine judgment of wicked men (2 Kings 1:10, 12, 14; Luke 9:54; 17:29).

**deceived** (v. 10)—Just as his demons will entice the world's armies into the Battle of Armageddon, Satan will draw them into a suicidal assault against Christ and His people (16:13–14).

**tormented day and night** (v. 10)—See 14:11. Continuous, unrelieved torment will be the final state of Satan, fallen angels, and unredeemed men.

**great white throne** (v. 11)—Nearly fifty times in Revelation there is the mention of a throne. This is a judgment throne, elevated, pure, and holy. God sits on it as judge (see 4:2–3, 9; 5:1, 7, 13; 6:16; 7:10, 15) in the person of the Lord Jesus Christ (see 21:5–6).

9 They went up on the breadth of the earth and surrounded the camp of the saints and the beloved city. And fire came down from God out of heaven and devoured them.

10 The devil, who deceived them, was cast into the lake of fire and brimstone where the beast and the false prophet are. And they will be tormented day and night forever and ever.

11 Then I saw a great white throne and Him who sat on it, from whose face the earth and the heaven fled away. And there was found no place for them.

12 And I saw the dead, small and great, standing before God, and books were opened. And another book was opened, which is the Book of Life. And the dead were judged according to their works, by the things which were written in the books.

13 The sea gave up the dead who were in it, and Death and Hades delivered up the dead who were in them. And they were judged, each one according to his works.

14 Then Death and Hades were cast into the lake of fire. This is the second death.

15 And anyone not found written in the Book of Life was cast into the lake of fire.

**earth and the heaven fled away** (v. 11)—John saw the contaminated universe go out of existence. Peter described this moment in 2 Peter 3:10–13. The universe is "uncreated," going into nonexistence.

**standing before God** (v. 12)—in a judicial sense, as guilty, condemned prisoners before the bar of divine justice; there are no living sinners left in the destroyed universe since all sinners were killed and all believers glorified

**books** (v. 12)—These books record every thought, word, and deed of sinful men—all recorded by divine omniscience (see Dan. 7:10, the verse that is the source of this text). They will provide the evidence for eternal condemnation (see 18:6–7).

**Book of Life** (v. 12)—It contains the names of all the redeemed (see 3:5).

**judged according to their works** (v. 12)—Their thoughts (Luke 8:17), words (Matt. 12:37), and actions (Matt. 16:27) will be compared to God's perfect, holy standard (Matt. 5:48) and will be found wanting (Rom. 3:23). This also implies that there are degrees of punishment in hell (see Matt. 10:14–15; 11:22; Mark 12:38–40; Luke 12:47–48).

**Death and Hades** (v. 13)—See 1:18. Both terms describe the state of death. All unrighteous dead will appear at the Great White Throne judgment; none will escape. All the places that have held the bodies of the unrighteous dead will yield up new bodies suited for hell.

1) What reasons are given for heaven's rejoicing in 19:1–5?

_____

_____

_____

_____

2) Why would the redeemed of heaven be glad for God's judgment?

_____

_____

_____

_____

*(Verses to consider: Isa. 9:7; Jer. 23:5; Rev. 16:7)*

3) What is "the marriage of the Lamb"?

_____

_____

_____

_____

*(Verses to consider: John 14:1–3; 2 Cor. 11:2; Eph. 1:4 ; 5:22–24)*

4) How is the Second Coming of Christ described by John in chapter 19?

_____

_____

_____

_____

*(Verses to consider: Matt. 24:27–31; Acts 1:9–11; 17:31)*

5) Compare and contrast the judgment of Satan with the reward of the faithful witnesses during the thousand years. What will God do (20:1–6)?

_____

_____

_____

6) Describe what will happen at the Great White Throne judgment. Who will be judged, and how?

_____

_____

_____

_____

_____

*(Verses to consider: Matt. 11:20–24; John 5:22–29; 12:48;*
*Acts 17:31; Rom. 2:5, 16; Heb. 9:27; 2 Pet. 2:9; 3:7; Jude 6)*

## GOING DEEPER

The prophet Micah foresaw the time when God would reign over all. Read Micah 4:1–8.

1 *Now it shall come to pass in the latter days that the mountain of the LORD's house shall be established on the top of the mountains, and shall be exalted above the hills; and peoples shall flow to it.*

2 *Many nations shall come and say, "Come, and let us go up to the mountain of the LORD, to the house of the God of Jacob; He will teach us His ways, and we shall walk in His paths." For out of Zion the law shall go forth, and the word of the LORD from Jerusalem.*

3 *He shall judge between many peoples, and rebuke strong nations afar off; they shall beat their swords into plowshares, and their spears into pruning hooks; nation shall not lift up sword against nation, neither shall they learn war anymore.*

4 *But everyone shall sit under his vine and under his fig tree, and no one shall make them afraid; for the mouth of the LORD of hosts has spoken.*

5 *For all people walk each in the name of his god, but we will walk in the name of the LORD our God forever and ever.*

6 *"In that day," says the LORD, "I will assemble the lame, I will gather the outcast and those whom I have afflicted;*

7 *I will make the lame a remnant, and the outcast a strong nation; so the LORD will reign over them in Mount Zion from now on, even forever.*

8 *And you, O tower of the flock, the stronghold of the daughter of Zion, to you shall it come, even the former dominion shall come, the kingdom of the daughter of Jerusalem."*

## Exploring the Meaning

7) How does the prophet Micah describe the coming Millennium time of peace?

_____

_____

_____

8) What will draw people to God's mountain?

_____

_____

_____

9) Read 2 Samuel 7:12–16. What promise did King David receive? How is it fulfilled in Jesus? Why is the premillennialist view necessary for the fulfillment of this prophecy?

_____

_____

_____

## Truth for Today

All attempts to equate this glorious reign of Christ over the whole earth with any past event or with the church is utterly foreign and contradictory to the clear eschatological teaching of Scripture. There is no way this text can be fulfilled except by the universal reign of Jesus Christ over the whole earth—as the prophets had for so long predicted.

## Reflecting on the Text

10) How does this glorious picture of Jesus' returning and making all things right encourage you? Do you still have questions about Christ's coming reign on earth? If so, write them out here.

_____

_____

_____

11) Which millennialist view of Christ's thousand-year reign do you support? Why?

_____

_____

_____

12) What hopes and fears do the truths of these two chapters bring to the surface in your own soul?

_____

_____

_____

13) List the names of friends, loved ones, neighbors, classmates, etc., who have not yet been confirmed as written in God's Book of Life. Ask God for the opportunity to use your relationship and example to point these people to Christ.

_____

_____

_____

## PERSONAL RESPONSE

Write out additional reflections, questions you may have, or a prayer.

_____

_____

_____

_____

_____

_____

_____

_____

_____

# 12

# ALL THINGS NEW
*Revelation 21:1–22:21*

## DRAWING NEAR

John closes his book with God's promise of a new heaven and a new earth. What do you think heaven will be like?

_____

_____

_____

Does the thought of eternity make you happy or fearful? Why?

_____

_____

_____

As we come to the end of this study, what new things have you learned about God?

_____

_____

_____

## THE CONTEXT

The ending of the book of Revelation is as dramatic and wonderful as the beginning. When the smoke clears following God's final punishment of the wicked, earth as we know it will be no more. John records in chapters 21–22 the startling revelation of the city of God and the beginning of the eternal state. Clearly, Paradise lost in the Garden of Eden (Gen. 3) will be Paradise regained! Satan, the beast, and false prophet, will be thrown into the lake of fire forever. God will create a new universe to be the eternal dwelling place of the redeemed. The citizens of eternity—Old Testament saints, Tribulation saints, and all those converted during the millennial kingdom—will dwell in the New Jerusalem, the heavenly city marked by the awesome glory and presence of God. Watch for themes that have been mentioned before: angels, the Lamb of God on the throne, the Book of Life, a lake of fire, a river of life.

The book began with the words of Jesus to the seven churches. It concludes with the penetrating words of Christ, the Alpha and Omega, the Morning Star. The Lord of life and King of eternity is coming soon! May our earnest and sincere prayer be the same as John's: "Amen. Even so, come, Lord Jesus!"

## KEYS TO THE TEXT

*New Jerusalem:* This is the capital city of heaven, a place of perfect holiness. It is seen "coming down out of heaven," indicating it already existed; but it descends into the new heavens and new earth from its place on high. This is the city where the saints will live (see John 14:1–3).

*The Bride:* This is an important New Testament metaphor for the church (Matt. 25:1–13; Eph. 5:25–27). John's imagery here extends from the third part of the Jewish wedding, the ceremony. Believers (the bride) in the New Jerusalem come to meet Christ (the bridegroom) in the final ceremony of redemptive history (see 19:7). The whole city, occupied by all the saints, is called the bride, so that all saints must be finally included in the bride imagery and bridal blessing. God has brought home a bride for His beloved Son. All the saints live with Christ in the Father's house (John 14:2).

## UNLEASHING THE TEXT

Read 21:1–22:21, noting the key words and definitions next to the passage.

### Revelation 21:1–22:21 (NKJV)

***a new heaven and a new earth*** (v. 1)—The entire universe as we now know it will be destroyed and be replaced by a new creation that will last forever. This is an Old Testament teaching, as well as a New Testament one.

***no more sea*** (v. 1)—Currently three-fourths of the earth's surface is water, but the new environment will no longer be water-based and will have completely different climatic conditions (see 22:1–2).

***the tabernacle of God*** (v. 3)—The word translated "tabernacle" means place of abode. This is God's house, the place where He lives.

1 Now I saw a new heaven and a new earth, for the first heaven and the first earth had passed away. Also there was no more sea.

2 Then I, John, saw the holy city, New Jerusalem, coming down out of heaven from God, prepared as a bride adorned for her husband.

3 And I heard a loud voice from heaven saying, "Behold, the tabernacle of God is with men, and He will dwell with them, and they shall be His people. God Himself will be with them and be their God.

4 And God will wipe away every tear from their eyes; there shall be no more death, nor sorrow, nor

***wipe away every tear*** (v. 4)—Since there will never be a tear in heaven, nothing will be sad, disappointing, deficient, or wrong.

crying. There shall be no more pain, for the former things have passed away."

5 Then He who sat on the throne said, "Behold, I make all things new." And He said to me, "Write, for these words are true and faithful."

6 And He said to me, "It is done! I am the Alpha and the Omega, the Beginning and the End. I will give of the fountain of the water of life freely to him who thirsts.

7 He who overcomes shall inherit all things, and I will be his God and he shall be My son.

8 But the cowardly, unbelieving, abominable, murderers, sexually immoral, sorcerers, idolaters, and all liars shall have their part in the lake which burns with fire and brimstone, which is the second death."

9 Then one of the seven angels who had the seven bowls filled with the seven last plagues came to me and talked with me, saying, "Come, I will show you the bride, the Lamb's wife."

10 And he carried me away in the Spirit to a great and high mountain, and showed me the great city, the holy Jerusalem, descending out of heaven from God,

11 having the glory of God. Her light was like a most precious stone, like a jasper stone, clear as crystal.

12 Also she had a great and high wall with twelve gates, and twelve angels at the gates, and names written on them, which are the names of the twelve tribes of the children of Israel:

13 three gates on the east, three gates on the north, three gates on the south, and three gates on the west.

14 Now the wall of the city had twelve foundations, and on them were the names of the twelve apostles of the Lamb.

15 And he who talked with me had a gold reed to measure the city, its gates, and its wall.

**true and faithful** (v. 5)—See 3:14; 19:11. God always speaks truth.

**water of life** (v. 6)—See 7:17; 22:1, 17. This refers to the lasting spiritual water of which Jesus spoke.

**him who thirsts** (v. 6)—Heaven belongs to those who, knowing their souls are parched by sin, have earnestly sought the satisfaction of salvation and eternal life.

**He who overcomes** (v. 7)—See 1 John 5:4–5. This refers to anyone who exercises saving faith in Jesus Christ (see 2:7).

**inherit** (v. 7)—The spiritual inheritance all believers will receive is the fullness of the new creation.

**shall have their part in the lake which burns** (v. 8)—This is a solemn, serious warning about the kinds of people who will be outcasts from the new heaven and the new earth in the lake of fire. The New Testament often goes beyond just citing unbelief in listing character and lifestyle traits of the outcast, so that believers can identify such people.

**the Lamb's wife** (v. 9)—The New Jerusalem takes on the character of its inhabitants, the redeemed (see v. 2; 19:7–9).

**jasper** (v. 11)—This is a transliteration, not a translation, of the Greek word. Rather than the modern opaque jasper, the term actually refers to a completely clear diamond, a perfect gem with the brilliant light of God's glory shining out of it and streaming over the new heaven and the new earth (see 4:3).

**gold reed** (v. 15)—The reed was about ten feet long, which was a standard of measurement.

**measure the city** (v. 15)—This action indicates that the capital of heaven belongs to God and He is measuring what is His (see 11:1).

**length, breadth, and height** (v. 16)—The city has the symmetrical dimensions of a perfect cube, which parallels its closest earthly counterpart, the inner sanctuary in the tabernacle and temple.

**twelve thousand furlongs** (v. 16)—This would be nearly fourteen hundred miles cubed or over two million square miles, offering plenty of room for all the glorified saints to live.

**one hundred and forty-four cubits** (v. 17)—Seventy-two yards or two hundred sixteen feet; likely the width of the wall

**jasper** (v. 18)—See verse 11. This is the material of the thick wall-diamond.

**pure gold, like clear glass** (v. 18)—Unlike earth's gold, this gold will be transparent so the over-powering radiance of God's glory can refract and glisten through the entire city.

16 *The city is laid out as a square; its length is as great as its breadth. And he measured the city with the reed: twelve thousand furlongs. Its length, breadth, and height are equal.*

17 *Then he measured its wall: one hundred and forty-four cubits, according to the measure of a man, that is, of an angel.*

18 *The construction of its wall was of jasper; and the city was pure gold, like clear glass.*

19 *The foundations of the wall of the city were adorned with all kinds of precious stones: the first foundation was jasper, the second sapphire, the third chalcedony, the fourth emerald,*

20 *the fifth sardonyx, the sixth sardius, the seventh chrysolite, the eighth beryl, the ninth topaz, the tenth chrysoprase, the eleventh jacinth, and the twelfth amethyst.*

21 *The twelve gates were twelve pearls: each individual gate was of one pearl. And the street of the city was pure gold, like transparent glass.*

**chalcedony** (v. 19)—This name derives from Chalcedon, an ancient name for a city in modern Turkey. The gem is a sky-blue agate stone with translucent, colored stripes.

**sardonyx** (v. 20)—a variety of chalcedony with parallel layers of red and white (see v. 19)

**sardius** (v. 20)—a common stone from the quartz family, which ranged in color from orange-red to brownish-red to blood-red (4:3)

**chrysolite** (v. 20)—a gem with a transparent gold or yellowish tone

**beryl** (v. 20)—a mineral with several varieties of gems, ranging from the green emerald to the golden yellow beryl to the light blue aquamarine

**topaz** (v. 20)—Ancient topaz was a softer stone with a yellow or yellow-green color.

**chrysoprase** (v. 20)—The modern form of this jewel is an apple-green variety of quartz. The Greek name suggests a gold-tinted, green gemstone.

**jacinth** (v. 20)—Today this stone is a transparent zircon, usually red or reddish-brown. The one John saw was blue or shining violet in color.

**amethyst** (v. 20)—A clear quartz crystal that ranges in color from a faint purple to an intense purple.

**one pearl** (v. 21)—Each of the gates of the city is a single, fifteen hundred-mile-high pearl. Even as earthly pearls are formed in response to the wounding of oyster flesh, so these gigantic, supernatural pearls will remind saints throughout eternity of the magnitude of Christ's suffering and its eternal benefit.

**22** But I saw no temple in it, for the Lord God Almighty and the Lamb are its temple.

**23** The city had no need of the sun or of the moon to shine in it, for the glory of God illuminated it. The Lamb is its light.

**24** And the nations of those who are saved shall walk in its light, and the kings of the earth bring their glory and honor into it.

**25** Its gates shall not be shut at all by day (there shall be no night there).

**26** And they shall bring the glory and the honor of the nations into it.

**27** But there shall by no means enter it anything that defiles, or causes an abomination or a lie, but only those who are written in the Lamb's Book of Life.

**22:1** And he showed me a pure river of water of life, clear as crystal, proceeding from the throne of God and of the Lamb.

**2** In the middle of its street, and on either side of the river, was the tree of life, which bore twelve fruits, each tree yielding its fruit every month. The leaves of the tree were for the healing of the nations.

**3** And there shall be no more curse, but the throne of God and of the Lamb shall be in it, and His servants shall serve Him.

**4** They shall see His face, and His name shall be on their foreheads.

**no temple** (v. 22)—Several passages affirm that there is a temple in heaven (3:12; 7:15; 11:19; 15:5). Here, it is clear there is none in eternity. How can this be? The temple is not a building; it is the Lord God Himself. Verse 23 continues the thought of no temple, except God and the Lamb. The glory of God that illuminates all heaven defines it as His temple. There is no need for a temple in the eternal state since God Himself will be the temple in which everything exists. The presence of God literally fills the entire new heaven and new earth (see v. 3). Going to heaven will be entering the limitless presence of the Lord.

**the nations** (v. 24)—Literally "the peoples," this means that the redeemed people from every nation and ethnic group will dwell in heaven's light. In the eternal city, there will be no more divisions, barriers, or exclusions because of race or politics. All kinds of peoples in eternity dissolve into the people of God, and they will move freely in and about the city.

**river . . . of life** (22:1)—This river is unlike any on earth because no hydrological cycle exists. Water of life symbolizes the continual flow of eternal life from God's throne to heaven's inhabitants (see 21:6).

**tree of life** (v. 2)—A symbol of both eternal life and continual blessing. The tree bears twelve fruits, one for each month, and is symbolic of the abundant variety in heaven. The English word "therapeutic" comes from the Greek word translated "healing." The leaves somehow enrich heavenly life, making it full and satisfying.

**no more curse** (v. 3)—The curse on humanity and the earth as a result of Adam and Eve's disobedience (Gen. 3:16–19) will be totally finished. God will never have to judge sin again, since it will never exist in the new heaven and new earth.

**see His face** (v. 4)—For all human history, no unglorified human could see God's face and live. But the residents of heaven can look on God's face without harm because they are now holy.

**His name** (v. 4)—They are God's personal possession (see 3:12).

*they shall reign* (v. 5)—Heaven's citizens are more than servants (see 3:21).

*His servants* (v. 6)—The members of the seven churches of Asia Minor who received this letter (1:11), and then all believers who have read or will read it since.

*things which must shortly take place* (v. 6)—This involves the entire revelation that John has just related (see 1:1).

*I am coming quickly!* (v. 7)—Jesus' return is imminent (see 3:11).

*heard and saw* (v. 8)—John resumes speaking for the first time since chapter 1 and confirms the veracity of the revelation with his own eyewitness testimony—the basis of any reliable witness.

*Do not seal the words* (v. 10)—See 10:11. Previous prophecies were sealed up. These prophecies are to be proclaimed so they can produce obedience and worship.

*the time is at hand* (v. 10)—This refers to imminency, which means that the end is next.

*according to his work* (v. 12)—Only those works which survive God's testing fire have eternal value and are worthy of reward.

*Blessed are those who do His commandments* (v. 14)—See 1:3. The preferred reading is "Blessed are those who wash their robes," symbolizing those who have been forgiven of their sins—who have been cleansed by the blood of the Lamb of God (Heb. 9:14; 1 Pet. 1:18–19; see 7:14).

5 There shall be no night there: They need no lamp nor light of the sun, for the Lord God gives them light. And they shall reign forever and ever.

6 Then he said to me, "These words are faithful and true." And the Lord God of the holy prophets sent His angel to show His servants the things which must shortly take place.

7 "Behold, I am coming quickly! Blessed is he who keeps the words of the prophecy of this book."

8 Now I, John, saw and heard these things. And when I heard and saw, I fell down to worship before the feet of the angel who showed me these things.

9 Then he said to me, "See that you do not do that. For I am your fellow servant, and of your brethren the prophets, and of those who keep the words of this book. Worship God."

10 And he said to me, "Do not seal the words of the prophecy of this book, for the time is at hand.

11 He who is unjust, let him be unjust still; he who is filthy, let him be filthy still; he who is righteous, let him be righteous still; he who is holy, let him be holy still."

12 "And behold, I am coming quickly, and My reward is with Me, to give to every one according to his work.

13 I am the Alpha and the Omega, the Beginning and the End, the First and the Last."

14 Blessed are those who do His commandments, that they may have the right to the tree of life, and may enter through the gates into the city.

15 But outside are dogs and sorcerers and sexually immoral and murderers and idolaters, and whoever loves and practices a lie.

16 "I, Jesus, have sent My angel to testify to you these things in the churches. I am the Root and the Offspring of David, the Bright and Morning Star."

*dogs* (v. 15)—Dogs were considered despicable creatures in New Testament times; when applied to people, the term referred to anyone of low moral character. Unfaithful leaders (Isa. 56:10) and homosexual prostitutes (Deut. 23:18) are among those who received such a designation.

*the churches* (v. 16)—the seven churches of Asia Minor which were the book's original recipients (1:11)

17 *And the Spirit and the bride say, "Come!" And let him who hears say, "Come!" And let him who thirsts come. Whoever desires, let him take the water of life freely.*

18 *For I testify to everyone who hears the words of the prophecy of this book: If anyone adds to these things, God will add to him the plagues that are written in this book;*

19 *and if anyone takes away from the words of the book of this prophecy, God shall take away his part from the Book of Life, from the holy city, and from the things which are written in this book.*

20 *He who testifies to these things says, "Surely I am coming quickly." Amen. Even so, come, Lord Jesus!*

21 *The grace of our Lord Jesus Christ be with you all. Amen.*

**the Root and the Offspring of David** (v. 16)—Christ is the source (root) of David's life and line of descendants, which establishes His deity. He is also a descendant of David (offspring), which establishes His humanity. This phrase gives powerful testimony to Christ as the God-Man (see 2 Tim. 2:8).

**Bright and Morning Star** (v. 16)—This is the brightest star announcing the arrival of the day. When Jesus comes, He will be the brightest star who will shatter the darkness of man's night and herald the dawn of God's glorious day (see 2:28).

**"Come!"** (v. 17)—This is the Spirit's and church's answer to the promise of His coming.

**let him** (v. 17)—This is an unlimited offer of grace and salvation to all who desire to have their thirsty souls quenched.

**"Surely I am coming quickly."** (v. 20)—See 3:11. In light of this future expectation, what is now required of believers is outlined by Peter (see 2 Pet. 3:11–18).

1) At the end of time, what will happen to this earth?

_____

_____

_____

_____

_____

(Verses to consider: Ps. 102:25–26; Isa. 65:17; Luke 21:33; Heb. 1:10–12; 2 Pet. 3:10–13)

2) How is the glory of the New Jerusalem described?

_____

_____

_____

_____

_____

133

3) What things will be banished from heaven (21:8, 27)?

_____

_____

_____

_____

4) Why is there no temple or need for light?

_____

_____

_____

_____

5) What does John say the inhabitants of heaven will be doing?

_____

_____

_____

_____

6) Skim the passage and list all the names for Jesus you can find. Which one has the most meaning for you right now?

_____

_____

_____

## DIGGING DEEPER

The Bible begins and ends with a perfect creation. In the beginning God set Adam and Eve in a beautiful garden. He dwelled with them in this paradise, and gave them only one rule: Don't eat of the tree of knowledge of good and evil. But then something went wrong. Read Genesis 3:1–24.

1   *Now the serpent was more cunning than any beast of the field which the LORD God had made. And he said to the woman, "Has God indeed said, 'You shall not eat of every tree of the garden'?"*

2   *And the woman said to the serpent, "We may eat the fruit of the trees of the garden;*

3   *but of the fruit of the tree which is in the midst of the garden, God has said, 'You shall not eat it, nor shall you touch it, lest you die.' "*

4   *Then the serpent said to the woman, "You will not surely die.*

5   *For God knows that in the day you eat of it your eyes will be opened, and you will be like God, knowing good and evil."*

6   *So when the woman saw that the tree was good for food, that it was pleasant to the eyes, and a tree desirable to make one wise, she took of its fruit and ate. She also gave to her husband with her, and he ate.*

7   *Then the eyes of both of them were opened, and they knew that they were naked; and they sewed fig leaves together and made themselves coverings.*

8   *And they heard the sound of the LORD God walking in the garden in the cool of the day, and Adam and his wife hid themselves from the presence of the LORD God among the trees of the garden.*

9   *Then the LORD God called to Adam and said to him, "Where are you?"*

10  *So he said, "I heard Your voice in the garden, and I was afraid because I was naked; and I hid myself."*

11  *And He said, "Who told you that you were naked? Have you eaten from the tree of which I commanded you that you should not eat?"*

12  *Then the man said, "The woman whom You gave to be with me, she gave me of the tree, and I ate."*

13  *And the LORD God said to the woman, "What is this you have done?" The woman said, "The serpent deceived me, and I ate."*

14  *So the LORD God said to the serpent: "Because you have done this, You are cursed more than all cattle, And more than every beast of the field; on your belly you shall go, and you shall eat dust all the days of your life.*

15  *And I will put enmity between you and the woman, and between your seed and her Seed; He shall bruise your head, and you shall bruise His heel."*

16  *To the woman He said: "I will greatly multiply your sorrow and your conception; in pain you shall bring forth children; your desire shall be for your husband, and he shall rule over you."*

17  *Then to Adam He said, "Because you have heeded the voice of your wife, and have eaten from the tree of which I commanded you, saying, 'You shall not eat of it': "Cursed is the ground for your sake; in toil you shall eat of it all the days of your life.*

18  *Both thorns and thistles it shall bring forth for you, and you shall eat the herb of the field.*

19  *In the sweat of your face you shall eat bread till you return to the ground, for out of it you were taken; for dust you are, and to dust you shall return."*

20 *And Adam called his wife's name Eve, because she was the mother of all living.*

21 *Also for Adam and his wife the LORD God made tunics of skin, and clothed them.*

22 *Then the LORD God said, "Behold, the man has become like one of Us, to know good and evil. And now, lest he put out his hand and take also of the tree of life, and eat, and live forever"—*

23 *therefore the LORD God sent him out of the garden of Eden to till the ground from which he was taken.*

24 *So He drove out the man; and He placed cherubim at the east of the garden of Eden, and a flaming sword which turned every way, to guard the way to the tree of life.*

## EXPLORING THE MEANING

7) What similarities do you find between the Garden of Eden and the new city of God in Revelation 22?

_____

_____

_____

_____

_____

8) In what specific ways will all the consequences of the Fall in the Garden of Eden be reversed in God's new heavenly kingdom (see Rev. 22)?

_____

_____

_____

9) Read John 4:13–14 and 7:37–38. What do these words of Jesus have to do with the "water of life" mentioned in Revelation 22?

_____

_____

_____

_____

10) Read Exodus 33:20–23. Moses wanted to see God. How is this scene different from what heaven will be like (see 21:3–4; 22:3–4)?

_____

_____

_____

_____

_____

*(Verses to consider: John 1:18; 1 Tim. 6:16)*

## TRUTH FOR TODAY

The Apocalypse reveals a great many divine truths. It warns the church of the danger of sin and instructs it about the need for holiness. It reveals the strength that Christ and believers have to overcome Satan. It reveals the glory and majesty of God and depicts the reverent worship that constantly attends His throne. The book of Revelation reveals the end of human history, including the final political setup of the world, the career of Antichrist, and the climactic Battle of Armageddon. It reveals the coming glory of Christ's earthly reign during the millennial kingdom, the Great White Throne judgment, and depicts the eternal bliss of the new heaven and the new earth. It reveals the ultimate victory of Jesus Christ over all human and demonic opposition. The book of Revelation describes the ultimate defeat of Satan and sin, and the final state of the wicked (eternal torment in hell) and the righteous (eternal joy in heaven). In short, it is the front-page story of the future of the world written by someone who has seen it all.

## REFLECTING ON THE TEXT

11) What part of heaven as described here is most surprising to you? What part do you most look forward to?

_____

_____

_____

_____

12) What does it mean to you that God will dwell with us in heaven, and will wipe away all tears and sorrow? How does that bring you strength and hope as you face the difficulties of life here on earth?

13) Jesus said, "Behold, I am coming quickly, and My reward is with Me, to give to every one according to his work" (22:12)? How does your life reflect a belief in that promise? How would your church be different if each member took this verse to heart?

*(Verses to consider: 1 Cor. 3:10–15; 4:1–5; 2 Cor. 5:10)*

14) In what three specific ways do you want your life to be different as a result of this study? Spend some time praising God, as the heavenly chorus did, for His goodness and power and holiness. Thank Him for the hope of heaven, and for all He has done for you through Jesus Christ.

## Personal Response

Write out additional reflections, questions you may have, or a prayer.

# Look for these exciting titles
# by John MacArthur

Available at your local Christian Bookstore
or visit www.thomasnelson.com